Light of the World

Light of the World

Daily Meditations for Advent

John Timmerman

LIGUORI, MISSOURI

Imprimi Potest: Thomas D. Picton, C.Ss.R.
Provincial, Denver Province • The Redemptorists

Published by Liguori Publications • Liguori, Missouri
www.liguori.org

Library of Congress Cataloging-in-Publication Data

Timmerman, John H.
Light of the world : daily meditations for Advent / John Timmerman. — 1st ed.
p. cm.
ISBN 978-0-7648-1621-5
1. Advent—Meditations. I. Title.
BV40.T56 2007
242′.332—dc22 2007016572

Liguori Publications, a nonprofit corporation, is an apostolate of the Redemptorists. To learn more about the Redemptorists, visit *Redemptorists.com.*

Printed in the United States of America
11 10 09 08 07 5 4 3 2 1
First edition

For my children—
Jeff, Betsy, Tamara, and Joel—
who made each Advent full of adventure.

CONTENTS

INTRODUCTION

I met him during that unusual span of days between Christmas and New Year. It always seemed to me that time itself gets oddly suspended then, as if the days are holding their breath. The great anticipation has come and gone; we only need the jump-start of January 1 to set the clock of our routine days going.

I met him at our local Veterans Counseling Center, where I have volunteered for the last seven or eight years to help jobless veterans prepare résumés and job applications. A fair percentage of these men are homeless, living in downtown shelters; nearly as many carry prison or jail records. Sometimes they call me when they get a job. Sometimes one will write a note of thanks. Most often we part ways when my work is done, and I never hear from them again.

Oddly, there has never been a call for my help during Christmas vacation. Factories and stores are laying off temporary help. The year closes down. The brief parties at the shelters and kitchens are all done now, and it's back to the standard fare. At such a time I met him.

He was a slightly overweight man, his eyes bruised by years of alcoholism. He told me that he had just finished the Salvation Army program—dry now for 192 days. I wondered if he would ever have to stop counting. It's a good program, I told him. I know others who have made it.

He nodded. We got to work. I went over papers, background, and abilities in preparation. Then he leaned back at one point and said to me, his eyes wistful, "You know, there ain't nothin' as over as Christmas."

I watched him for a moment to see if he would want to follow up. But he let the words hang there in the air, where they seemed to deflate gradually like balloons with a slow leak. When we finished our work, I was surprised that I carried his words away with me.

There ain't nothin' as over as Christmas. At the end of a long acceleration, we cross the finish line. Wrappers and boxes are stuffed into garbage bags; leftover food is consigned to the freezer or the disposal.

It's done.

Somewhere along the way, we make time to read the Christmas story, perhaps more than once. In churches we sing the carols, light the Advent candles. We return to our homes where anticipation mounts like the spreading ring of presents under the tree. Of course we celebrate, and it is good that we celebrate. It is our feast day over glad tidings.

But then: *There ain't nothin' as over as Christmas.*

Why? Because if we measure Christmas by our human investment, it will always wind up as a losing proposition. We will forever be like the child who didn't quite get the gift he or she wanted and will feel a little cheated, a little empty. Something will be missing.

That something, of course, will be the renewal of our love for Jesus, which isn't ever over at Christmas but grows greater, with passionate intensity, each year. Sometimes we feel like we love especially dear persons—a spouse, or friend, or parent, for example—more every time we meet them. This is a mirror to our loving Jesus. However, just as we have to come into the presence of our spouse or friend or parent in order to nurture that love, so too we have to come into the presence of Jesus.

Some of those human relationships, moreover, can deepen so powerfully, becoming such an intimate part of who we are, that neither change nor distance can ever sever them. Our intimacy with Jesus is like that also: "...[N]either death, nor life, nor angels, nor rulers, nor things present, nor things to come, nor powers, nor height, nor depth, nor anything else in all creation, will be able to separate us from the love of God in Christ Jesus our Lord"

(Romans 8:38). That is a relationship that is never *over.* It endures well past the ceremonies and festivities. Temporary celebration is a candle to the pure floodlight of joy.

To participate in it, however, we have to acquire that deep, sustaining knowledge and love of Jesus that cannot be contained simply in ceremonies. Without that, Christmas is just "over" on December 26. It dawns on an uneasy hollowness—"Well, that's done. Now what to do for fun?"

My purpose in writing this book is a simple one—to join with you in a more intimate understanding of and love for Jesus. The two always seem to work together intricately. It is very hard, after all, to love someone whom you do not know very well. Furthermore, Jesus himself has told us how to love him—"with all [our] heart, and with all [our] soul, and with all [our] mind, and with all [our] strength" (Mark 12:30). *Mind* is an interesting word there. It points to the fact that all those who love Jesus want to reflect on and meditate on this Lord whom we love.

The overwhelming thing about all this is that Jesus unwrapped mystery from himself as God, and tottered into this world in all his exposed infant humanity in order to reveal himself. We don't have to sit yogalike in the backyard trying to connect with some transcendental, mystical fuzz; we have a reality to examine. This is the God incarnate, the basis for our celebration as Christians, and the reason why, for believers, it ain't never over.

Because that presence of Jesus is so firmly and intimately a part of our present reality (not just that of the first century), our pursuit of knowing him better will follow a course of several names given prophetically to Jesus in the Old Testament or that Jesus ascribed to himself in the New Testament. Our method here, then, is similar to that of my earlier book of meditations for the Lenten season, *Woman, Why Are You Weeping?* (Liguori Publications, 2007). Furthermore, we will also consider several important people in Jesus' life who reveal much about our Redeemer.

By studying these names that apply particularly to the advent of our Savior, our purpose is not simply learning what to call someone, but understanding who that someone is. To know Jesus as Lord, the

God incarnate, and to understand that with him Christmas is never over, we'll study several of those important revelations.

We call our season of Christmas the Advent season. *Advent* itself is an interesting word. The Latin root simply means "arrival," but gradually it took on the meaning of the arrival of someone or something extremely important—an era, or person, or invention that changed history. In Christianity, the Advent season refers to a liturgical period of preparation (often through meditation and prayer) for the coming of Christ, beginning on the fourth Sunday before Christmas. So too we want to prepare our hearts through these meditations—getting ready to meet Jesus.

John Timmerman

First Week in Advent

First Sunday in Advent

MARY—BLESSED MOTHER

Since the Medieval period, they called her the Madonna—"the mother." The reason was simple. Few books existed, and very few people could read at all. Instead, their books were paintings—visual representations. They knew Mary through the works and imaginations of artists, and they were vivid representations indeed. In almost all of them, Mary is shown with the infant cradled on her lap. The mother.

These paintings, some done for cathedrals and some for private collections, all speak to the honor we still show Mary. Gabriel greeted her as the "favored one" and said "The Lord is with you" (Luke 1:28–29). Elizabeth added her praise: "Blessed are you among women, and blessed is the fruit of your womb" (Luke 1:42). Medieval artists tried to convey this honor, favor, and blessing to their viewers. The paintings range from relatively simple works to elaborately detailed works where Mary and Jesus are surrounded by heavenly hosts with Mary garbed in stunningly beautiful garments. In each instance, the artist tries to put a face on the divine mother whom we honor.

We still want to capture that honor. We call Mary, the mother of Jesus, by names of adoration—"Blessed Virgin" or "Blessed Lady"—for example. Mary inspired the music of Franz Schubert, whose "Ave Maria" seems to soar to the throne of heaven. It is fitting during this Advent season that we too have those words in our hearts:

Ave Maria, gratia plena.
Hail Mary, full of grace.

But just *why* do we honor Mary?

This woman we honor does not bear an unusual name in Scripture. Moses' sister was named Miriam, the Hebrew equivalent for the New Testament Mary. And Jesus' life was surrounded by others who bore the name: Mary the sister of Martha, Mary Magdalene, Mary the Mother of James, and others. But our Mary is special. Theologians love to speculate on her age, on her appearance, and on her attitude. We do know that Mary was a young woman of unparalleled faith. Gabriel appeared to her with the announcement:

> *"[Y]ou will conceive in your womb and bear a son, and you will name him Jesus. He will be great, and will be called the Son of the Most High, and the Lord God will give to him the throne of his ancestor David. He will reign over the house of Jacob forever, and of his kingdom there will be no end."*
>
> *LUKE 1:31–33*

There would be no doubt in Mary's mind, as there is no doubt in ours, that this Jesus was the Messiah of the world.

How would you have reacted? "You've got to be kidding? This is some kind of weird dream? I must have had too much sun!"

What does Mary say? Here are her words of faith: "Here am I, the servant of the Lord; let it be with me according to your word" (Luke 1:38). Mary leaves me speechless with her great faith. What pure and brave faith! Let no one call this "simple" faith. It was complete and powerful—thorough in agreement and purpose.

Mary—our mother of faith. So we meet Mary again at Advent, and learn from her. But faith is not her only lesson, not the only reason we honor her so highly.

Another important lesson from Mary is her great joy. I can only imagine what things she "pondered in her heart." No, I really can't. Did she sense the conflict of the Messiah within her? Could she sense the implications of carrying God in her womb? It beggars my poor imagination. But this we know—Mary was a woman of joy.

Filled with the Holy Spirit, Elizabeth exclaims, "Why has this happened to me, that the mother of my Lord comes to me?" (Luke 1:43). Look how Mary reacts. She bursts into song:

My soul magnifies the Lord,
and my spirit rejoices in God my Savior,
for he has looked with favor on the lowliness of his servant.

LUKE 1:46–48

For three months the two expectant mothers, Elizabeth and Mary, lived together. And we expect that they did all those motherly things—give reports, talk, compare foods—that any new mother does. They also rejoiced. But what happens to rejoicing when the trials come? How important that question is when we look at the final reason why we honor Mary.

Mary's life would not have been easy. Shortly after Jesus' birth, Joseph and Mary learned of Herod's edict to slaughter all male children younger than the age of two years. Could they have lost their baby…and all their joy? Understand that Mary and Joseph were what we might call "dirt poor." Yes, they could afford the offering of two doves when Jesus was consecrated on the eighth day, but hardly a long journey to escape Herod. Here God's miraculous hand intervenes, for the gifts of the Magi sustained them in Egypt for the two-year duration of Herod's decree. But imagine the terror in Mary—"I almost lost my child."

Mary also thought she had lost her son when he was twelve. After searching desperately for him, she found him at the Temple. Can you imagine her frantic sense of loss and final relief? How often don't we feel we are losing sons or daughters?

And finally, Mary was there, faithful and steadfast, but not rejoicing at all this time, when her son was crucified. There was nowhere to run now for Mary—or for her son. There was no last-minute intervention and deliverance, for her own son was intervening for delivering her. This is the way God planned it, Mary. Maybe she wanted to forget Gabriel's words then. He is the Son of God. Can God really die? Only if God himself willed it so, and only, *only* if he had been born to the Virgin Mary, taking on human flesh, and being Mary's son at the very same moment he is the Son of God.

Hail, Mary. Full of grace. Indeed. But Mary is so much more than the Blessed Virgin, so much more than the many names we bestow on her to honor her. Along with her son Jesus, Mary is the very model for us of how to live with faith and joy in a world that whirls with furious uncertainties.

Isaiah 7:14

> "Therefore the Lord himself will give you a sign. Look, the young woman is with child and shall bear a son, and shall name him Immanuel."

Prayer

Thank you, Lord,
for the expectation of this Advent season.
As the Old Testament prophet
waited the coming of the Immanuel,
the "God with Us"—our Savior—
may we rejoice in the knowledge
that he has come.
Give us the faith and joy
of Mary, Lord, as we celebrate
God among us.
Amen.

First Monday

THE FORERUNNER

Somehow, John the Baptist seems to get lost in the shuffle of events in Jesus' life. When we do remember him, it is likely for two very important events. First, he was the one who baptized his cousin Jesus in the Jordan River. Second, John was one of the first martyrs, slain for chastising King Herod for taking his brother Philip's wife, Herodias (see Matthew 14:1–12). If we try to picture John, we form an image of a desert wanderer, an itinerant preacher, dressed in camelhair bound with a leather belt. His hair was all unruly, his beard unshaven. The only baths he took were when he baptized people. All in all, not a figure we would want to cuddle up with on Christmas Eve. Truly the Lord makes use of the most uncomely and low among us, for John's task was announced from the throne of God himself.

The biblical record gives us much more to build on to see John's essential role in establishing the kingdom of God on this earth. It started with his father, Zechariah, a priest serving in the Temple. Zechariah was astonished at the sudden appearance of Gabriel, standing to one side of the altar. Once Gabriel quieted Zechariah's fears, he relayed a message from God about the child Elizabeth would bear.

Now, angels don't prophesy. That's a human task. Gabriel in particular serves as a direct messenger from God. He reveals immediate truth about something. In his address to Zechariah, Gabriel in fact proclaims five distinct truths about John's work. Following these, we see past the unruly garb of the desert vagabond to his holy and dangerous mission.

Gabriel first assures Zechariah about this child, born in the old age of his parents, "You will have joy and gladness, and many will rejoice at his birth" (Luke 1:14). Yes, the boy will bring joy to his parents. That is always good news. But how will he bring joy to *many*?

The answer lies in the second truth: "He will be great in the sight of the Lord" (Luke 1:15). Again, virtually anyone can take both solace and joy by being told their child will be great in the sight of the Lord. I imagine that Zechariah especially, as a priest in the Temple, must have beamed. What a blessing! But just how will this "greatness" appear?

The next truth fuses two qualities together and begins to define John's greatness: "He must never drink wine or strong drink; even before his birth he will be filled with the Holy Spirit" (Luke 1:15). Forsaking wine and drink were the marks of the Nazarites, a priestly people set apart for God. The progression here, though, is interesting. Instead of wine, John will be filled with the Holy Spirit.

The fourth task relays John's mission, his peculiar calling in God's kingdom: "He will turn many of the people of Israel to the Lord their God" (Luke 1:16). Thereby, John is allied with the tradition of the prophets, calling God's chosen people back to him. In large part, John enacts this truth in his twofold mission of evangelizing and baptizing.

The fifth truth, however, broadens John's mission: "With the spirit and power of Elijah he will go before him, to turn the hearts of parents to their children, and the disobedient to the wisdom of the righteous, to make ready a people prepared for the Lord" (Luke 1:17). There lies John's mission as the Christmas servant. To be sure, Jesus' public ministry started when he was about thirty, but even before then, John preached the coming of the Messiah: "[O]ne who is more powerful than I is coming; I am not worthy to untie the thong of his sandals" (Luke 3:16). Before John was imprisoned by Herod, that day arrived. John was preaching and baptizing at the

Jordan River, when Jesus appeared through the crowd. Immediately John recognized his spiritual superior: "I need to be baptized by you," John exclaims, "and do you come to me?" (Matthew 3:14). Imagine, if you can, the reaction of a parish priest celebrating the sacrament when suddenly the archbishop walks in and kneels before him. Wouldn't his hands shake just slightly? For all of John's rough and tough words and actions, when the moment came, something like that must have struck him.

The miracle that follows beggars the human imagination. "[S]uddenly the heavens were opened" (Matthew 3:16). What does that mean? Did clouds and all space suddenly scroll back—as it did at Jesus' birth and as it did not at his death—and the glory of the Lord shine down? A dove appeared, and with it a voice: "This is my Son, the Beloved, with whom I am well pleased" (Matthew 3:17).

In a sense, John's work is done. He has fulfilled Gabriel's truths about his future. He could rest now and let his cousin Jesus carry on his own work.

John didn't see it that way. This messenger of God spoke the truth until he wound up in Herod's prison. The dusty, ragtag, camel's-hair life of John leaves an important message. We also have a task to speak the truth. Our message is precisely the same as John's: to testify to the coming of Jesus—"to make ready a people prepared for the Lord" (Luke 1:17).

Isaiah 40:3–5

A voice cries out:
"In the wilderness prepare the way of the LORD,
  make straight in the desert a highway for our God.
Every valley shall be lifted up,
  and every mountain and hill be made low;
the uneven ground shall become level,
  and the rough places a plain.
Then the glory of the LORD shall be revealed,
  and all people shall see it together,
  for the mouth of the LORD has spoken."

Prayer

Perhaps through John's eyes
I can get a glimpse
of Jesus. I am not worthy
to untie the thongs of his sandals either,
but look! Heaven breaks open,
God's voice sounds a blessing,
the dove settles toward Jesus.
What is this? Who is this?
The One who takes away
the sins of the world.
Like the flowing water
of the River Jordan, Lord,
wash over me,
anoint me with joy
I pray.
Amen.

First Tuesday

A GREAT CLOUD OF WITNESSES

Jesus did not spring into this world like some mysterious alien. He came with a history rooted in both eternity and in human time that was fully recognized at his birth. Therefore, we recognize those historical testimonies of such persons as Elizabeth, Mary, Gabriel, and John as testimonies to the truth. This is God's son, born as a human son.

We could include additional voices as witness bearers. Righteous Simeon, for example, had a revelation from the Holy Spirit that he would not die before he had seen the Lord's Christ (see Luke 2:26). Simeon did not doubt the voice, but simply stood prepared for its fulfillment at the only reasonable place—the Temple courts. We don't know how long he waited there, how many days or years. We know only that Simeon was faithful and full of belief. He waited.

His reward came on the day Joseph and Mary presented Jesus for consecration at the Temple. There stood Simeon in the court, peering out over any number of people coming and going. His eyes, directed by the Holy Spirit, fixed on the young couple, Mary and Joseph. He lifted their child in his arms, and he lifted praise to God and prophecy to the parents.

His historic testimony underlines all that we have heard previously:

"Master, now you are dismissing your servant in peace,
according to your word;
for my eyes have seen your salvation,
which you have prepared in the presence of all peoples,
a light for revelation to the Gentiles
and for glory to your people Israel."

LUKE 2:29–32

In our courts of law, when several persons independently testify to the same conditions of an event, each testimony is considered a corroboration of the truth. Here Simeon's words not only corroborate the other New Testament voices we have listened to, but also a whole choir of voices echoing through centuries of the Old Testament.

Yet another witness stands nearby in the temple court. Perhaps she doesn't look like much to human consideration. She is, after all, an eighty-four-year-old widow—exceedingly old given the average life span of this time. We can rightly imagine her as small and wrinkled. But we remember that God can pack a lot of power into some very small things. He had already done that in a manger in Bethlehem. So, too, God had packed his spirit into this prophetess named Anna.

Many prophetesses appeared in Jewish history. The Bible familiarizes us with Miriam, Deborah, and Huldah. Hannah, the Old Testament equivalent for "Anna," praised God for the birth of Samuel, just as Anna praises God for the birth of Jesus. Anna also bore witness to "all who were looking for the redemption of Jerusalem" (Luke 2:38).

It is an amazing scene really. Joseph and Mary come to the Temple, apparently to fulfill custom before setting out on their way. But there they are met with testimony and witnesses they did not expect. Can there be any doubts now? This child, consecrated to God now, is also God himself.

John 1:32–34

And John testified, "I saw the Spirit descending from heaven like a dove, and it remained on him. I myself did not know him, but the one who sent me to baptize with water said to me, 'He on whom you see the Spirit descend and remain is the one who baptizes with the Holy Spirit.' And I myself have seen and have testified that this is the Son of God."

Prayer

Lord,
what excitement there must have been
in the Temple that day.
It started with just routine offerings,
a tradition followed.
But surely others overheard Simeon,
and Anna made her praise known
to anyone she could find.
What strange and wonderful news
they spread:
Here in the House of God
is God himself;
the very One we make offerings to.
Oh, Holy God, Father, Son, and Holy Spirit,
with the voices of all these witnesses
will you please imprint these truths
to which they testified
afresh upon my heart.
Amen.

First Wednesday

THE PRINCE OF DARKNESS

There is one further witness to the Messiah whom we must consider here. He is one never mentioned, to my knowledge, in Advent stories. Indeed, we seldom like to mention him at all. Yet he is, indisputably, a part of the story. We cannot ignore him and still recognize the full meaning of the Advent. This figure stood at the advent of Jesus' earthly ministry.

In all versions of Scripture he is named the devil, the tempter figure whom we also know as Satan. This is the same devil who tempted Eve; the same one spoken of by John (see 1 John 3:8); the same one spoken of in Revelation (see 12:9). And now he appears to Jesus as recorded in Matthew (see 4:1–11).

This is not Jesus' first contact with Satan. In Luke 10, we find Jesus' commission to the seventy disciples who would go ahead of him preparing the way in every town he would visit. Jesus visits upon these disciples his own authority: "Whoever listens to you listens to me, and whoever rejects you rejects me, and whoever rejects me rejects the one who sent me" (v. 16). Could it be any clearer than that?

Perhaps it has to be. Sometime later these seventy return to Jesus ("with joy") and announce that "Lord, in your name even the demons submit to us!" (v. 17). Jesus' response, however, grips our attention: "I watched Satan fall from heaven like a flash of lightning" (v. 18). This is an amazing thing and in their joy the seventy may not even have caught the full meaning. If you, Jesus, saw it, does that mean you were in heaven? Yes, Jesus did see him fall from heaven, when Jesus was in heaven. Satan's crime and the necessity of his expulsion are made clear by Isaiah. Satan wanted to be like God, the very thing by which he tempted Adam and Eve. Here's Isaiah (14:12):

> *How you are fallen from heaven,*
> *O Day Star, son of Dawn!*
> *How you are cut down to the ground,*
> *you who laid the nations low!*

Nothing created can be higher than the Creator; therefore, the angel of light was cast from heaven and became the Prince of Darkness.

Now Jesus is about to start his ministry on earth in human form, subject to all the temptations that humans confront ("Because he himself was tested by what he suffered, he is able to help those who are being tested" Hebrews 2:18). The temptations recorded in Matthew 4:1–11 and Luke 4:1–13 take three primary forms. They come at the end of Jesus' forty days of fasting in the wilderness, the point where he was at his human weakest. Each temptation—turning rocks to bread to satisfy hunger, using his divine powers to save himself, and seizing political power over all the kingdoms of the world—appeal to some fundamental human desire. As the writer of Hebrews put it, "For we do not have a high priest who is unable to sympathize with our weaknesses, but we have one who in every respect has been tested as we are, yet without sin" (4:15).

If the first important lesson of the wilderness is that Jesus withstood temptation in fully human form, the second lesson is that he used the weapon available to any human believer—the word of God. Jesus never argues with Satan here; there is no need. He simply quotes Scripture, the unassailable word of God. Each time Jesus says, "It is written," and the Old Testament verses he cites destroy the Tempter.

The Advent of Jesus' birth, which we now celebrate, focuses on the miracle of God born as a baby in Bethlehem. But there was another advent some thirty years later, when this grown child began his ministry among humans to redeem them from the curse of sin. Not surprisingly, this was marked by a confrontation with the Sin-Bringer—Satan himself.

The Prince of Darkness still throws his shadow over this life, and over the lives of believers. But because Jesus defeated him at this second advent, we have the full security and certain knowledge of Jesus' power with us until death and the devil are forever destroyed.

Revelation 20:10

> And the devil who had deceived them was thrown into the lake of fire and sulfur, where the beast and the false prophet were, and they will be tormented day and night forever and ever.

Prayer

I cannot resist Satan's temptations,
not in my own strength.
I fall and fall again in the struggle.
I am ashamed of my failures
and the hurt I cause your holiness, Lord.
How thankful I am that you have overcome
for me, both in heaven and on earth.
Please, Lord, make your word so powerful
and alive in me that it will be a strong,
double-edged sword, defeating temptation,
staying the wiles of Satan,
keeping me alive in you.
Amen.

First Thursday

In the Thick of Darkness

I have never been brave against the dark. I do not mean the dark of night, understand. Although when I was very young and had to baby-sit for my younger brother and sister, I was sure that creatures scratched against the windows and I wanted to bury my head in the pillow and pretend I was asleep.

I love to be in the great darkness of the outdoors. It may be by a campfire in Colorado. It may be at the cabin in North Carolina where my wife and I like to sit on the porch swing, drinking coffee and watching fireflies poke holes in the night. And every night at bedtime I rouse our aging Sheltie and walk outside, watching the stars as distant as light-years, almost close enough to touch.

No. What I mean is the darkness that drives into the heart with icicle points and makes your breath catch in your throat. I have had several such times in my life, when I felt that fear is sucking my life out. It is fear in the presence of evil, when I felt the dark shadow of Satan's wings hover close and the claws open.

When I graduated from the Ph.D. program, armed with all my youthful enthusiasm, a love for teaching, and a wonderful and growing family, I was blessed to get a position at a Christian college. That was where I wanted to teach; I wasn't interested in a big university.

I wanted to exercise my faith and touch lives. The years we spent at that college were, for the most part, wonderful and exhilarating. We made friends we still hold dear. The teaching was challenging and stimulating. The small town and the college campus were among the most lovely and idyllic I have ever seen.

Most important, the new president of the college had been given a mandate by the board of trustees to recapture and revitalize the college's Christian tradition, much of which had slipped into mere relativism during the previous decade. Moreover, I learned, certain faculty members were not merely relativistic in their belief systems, but firmly opposed to Christianity. How opposed I was soon to learn.

If you want to change things in higher education, you do so by hiring new faculty and implementing a new curriculum. I was among that vanguard of new, young faculty—confident, eager, unafraid. For the most part.

Since we also arrived fresh out of graduate school and with no money for a down payment on a house, we were provided a large, decrepit old house on the college campus as our residence for a very nominal rent. We tried to brighten it up, but it was hopeless: high ceilings and huge spaces; loose paneling and brick falling from its three stories. Drafts curled across the hardwood floors. The furnace just couldn't drive out the constant chill. The room I used for a study was unheated altogether. With a space heater blasting, I worked wearing a coat as winter settled in. Since we had a dog with a bladder problem at the time, he slept in my study. I awakened one morning to find all my notes for the day shredded and dampened. We eventually gave the dog to a farm couple.

We were seated at the dinner table one evening when Betsy, a toddler of eighteen months, came screaming into the room. She had pulled a closet hanger entirely through her lower lip where it now dangled like some macabre appendage streaming blood. "I didn't do it," she wailed. Well then, who did? And where did she get the hanger? They were high in the closet.

The house was never warm. The kids caught chills, flu, and fever. I began to look for a house to buy. Anything we could afford. I would settle for a warm garage.

Then the sounds started. Footsteps, rather. Three bedrooms and a bathroom branched off a long hallway on the second story. The footsteps were heavy, very heavy as they paced from the kids' bedrooms toward the bathroom. Pat and I were instantly awake. "Who's there?" I shouted. I got up, flung open the door, turned on the light, and looked up and down the hallway. Nothing. I searched the downstairs. Nothing. Nothing but a vague disturbing fear.

There were other disturbing events. Like the bat that came out of nowhere one night flickering over our dinner table. For two weeks we didn't see it. Then it was there again, over the dinner table. I didn't want my children to witness their father's fury, but I ripped the cushion off the chair, swatted the bat out of the air, and stomped on it.

"Was that a bird, Daddy?" Betsy asked.

"No, honey. It was a bat."

"Oh. A bad bird."

It was then, as the season turned toward Christmas, that we learned that the previous tenants of the house, who were asked to leave so that we could live there temporarily (for which the college-owned house was kept), were Satanists. They held séances in the house, worked dark magic. And, we were led to understand, they had left curses on the house to attack these young Christians.

Fear began to grip us every time we stepped in. Then one night the footsteps again. Not in the hallway but in the third-story attic—slow, ponderous, wandering. I leapt out of bed, stormed up the stairs to the third floor, and shouted at the top of my lungs, "In the name of the Father and the Son and the Holy Spirit, get out of here!" Silence descended, but, oh, the darkness was thick. I wanted to slam my fists against something, but there seemed to be only silent mockery.

It was only a day or two later that the pastor of the church we had been attending stopped by. He had a large, wrapped package under his arm. The thought suddenly struck me, why hadn't I called him before? Because we were too new here…the story too bleak and strange…this didn't happen to normal Christians…because,

because. He knew the story, he said. It didn't surprise him at all. He knew what had happened here before.

Some Christian friends also came over. We prayed together. We gave everything—the work, the fear, the darkness—over to Jesus. I literally felt his light and love flood through me.

We opened the package. Inside was our first Advent wreath. We had never had one before—didn't even know how to use it. Our pastor explained the simple steps and the significance of each aspect of the wreath. The wreath is a circle, with no beginning and no ending. It symbolizes the eternal God. The four purple candles represent the four Sundays before Advent. They are the color of royalty. We prepare to meet our Messiah King. And the central candle of pure white? That stands in the center. That is the Christ candle positioned at the center of God's love and right in the midst of our four candles of human time.

Shortly after that we found our own home to buy. It wasn't a garage, but it didn't cost much. The next summer the college demolished the old house for a parking lot.

And that Advent wreath may look a little more tattered now when we unpack it each year. This will be its thirty-fifth year. But its meaning is eternal. There is a light that no darkness can overcome. It is good to remember.

John 14:27

> "Peace I leave with you; my peace I give to you. I do not give to you as the world gives. Do not let your hearts be troubled, and do not let them be afraid."

Prayer

Jesus my Lord, and Lord over every inch of your creation,
thank you for your victory over the darkness,
and for your grace and light which have set me free.
How I love your perfect peace.
Keep me safe there, I pray.
Amen.

First Friday

Longing for the Light

Let's consider the previous meditation just a bit further. Jesus came into this world to deliver us from fear and darkness. That's the great truth. Peter wrote the young church, "But even if you do suffer for doing what is right, you are blessed. Do not fear what they fear, and do not be intimidated" (1 Peter 3:14). And John, in his epistles of love, wrote that "perfect love casts out fear" (1 John 4:18). That "perfect love" alive in us is the love of Christ.

Yet, many of us have found ourselves breathing that bewildering "why" into a world made of shadows. Like the sickening weight of dread, a slow panic pounds through the whole body. It starts cramped in the chest and pulses heavily outward, like a crippled sparrow trying to fly.

It would be foolish of me to try to name the causes or the experiences for others. But many of us have had it; we say, "Yes, I know that feeling." Indeed, for some it is a nearly daily terror, waiting there the moment one steps out of bed. It becomes so very hard to explain, even when causes are clear, as they so seldom are.

I know. The trouble is that it can fall so unexpectedly.

If we are, as the psalmist says, fearfully and wonderfully made, sometimes we are too often aware of the fearful. The "why's" sometimes stack up in staggering proportions, mountains far too high for us to climb as we cower in the shadowed valleys.

I think of some of the why's in my own life. I wonder why my niece, just a month after giving her life to Jesus, was brutally murdered and her one-year-old daughter abducted. I wonder why members in our family suffer from depressive disorders, that illness that paints the mind in shades of gray and makes the world seem like a swamp through which one moves in slow motion. I wonder why the people who frequent a medical clinic where my wife volunteers as a nurse wander helpless and hopeless on the dark streets of the inner city. The "why's" rise for nearly each and every one of us.

My father, a wise man if I ever knew one, once said to me, "I don't trust a man who has never suffered." He pondered a bit, then added, "I don't trust a man who never laughs either."

Every human, as an old but profitable analogy has it, has been born with a hollow space in his or her heart. Some of the earliest theologians spoke of it as a desire. It can turn either toward the city of God or toward the city of the world. None of us escapes it. In some people, it seems that hole has deepened profoundly, the walls scarred like chiseled limestone, by events often beyond their control. It may be grief; it may be abuse in all its terrible levels from neglect to sexual; it may be an event so terrifying or threatening that the memory keeps hammering away at the hole to bury these things. Finally, the hole seems so deep the person caves in and falls down into its seemingly infinite blackness.

That hole is our need.

Many try to satisfy that need by narcotizing agents—drugs, alcohol, sex, money, power, to name a few. They are all deceitful agents, because they only draw a temporary veil over the hole while it keeps getting deeper. We try to fill an infinite space with finite means. It can only be filled by an infinite answer to need; the only such answer, I have found, is Jesus Christ in whom all things are made new. Only an infinite Lord can repair the damage.

This is not the belief of the world at large. In fact, many scoff at the notion as a delusion. For me, it is the essential premise in telling the true story of one's life. True stories are seldom neat and lovely; they seldom come in colors like designer clothing and words like bright ribbons. They are often messy, where words work hard at once to contest and also to convey the pain. But in telling the truth we can find the reality that begins to lead us out of the darkness. We can find the light that first illumines the hole in our hearts, and then begins to fill it.

The wonder of Advent is that we know where to look to find this light. It is not the piercing, mocking spotlight that exposes all our fears and darkness. Rather, it is light like a warm bath, flowing inside to wash away the darkness—a light of comfort and compassion.

Advent is the season of lights. No doubt the light has been commercialized into gaudy dazzle, one house or store trying desperately to outdo another. But that's only a perversion of an underlying reality. Since earliest times, in secret rooms or distant places, people huddled around candles for the warmth of the Christ. They have ringed Advent wreaths in adoration. They have welcomed the Light of the World.

The truly amazing thing for us is that this Light has already come to us, with welcome in his arms. There we can find comfort from the bewildering why's, hope that battles the shadows, and a true story that leads to an eternal joy.

Isaiah 25:7–8a

And he will destroy on this mountain
 the shroud that is cast over all peoples,
 the sheet that is spread over all nations;
 he will swallow up death forever.
Then the Lord GOD will wipe away the tears from all faces.

Prayer

Oh, Sovereign Lord.
How we long to have that shroud of darkness
removed from people and nations.
Free us from wars and rumors of wars.
Deliver us from the terror
that strikes even at noontime.

And when the darkness falls within,
clotting and shadowing our deepest joy,
we pray to you for the deliverance of your Light.
No darkness can stand against you.
Give us comfort; give us hope;
give us the sure understanding
that we belong to you now and for all eternity.
Amen.

First Saturday

SEARCHING THE MYSTERY OF JESUS

Simply because we cannot fully wrap our minds around the mystery of God the Father, we often think of him as the great "Unknowable." When God named himself to Moses as "I Am That I Am," we shake our heads. All the linguistic and theological studies in the world can't seem to contain the full scope of that. Like looking hard into space, we get lost in the dizzying flare of ever more distant constellations. Where does it all end?

On the other hand, because Jesus walked on this dusty earth in Palestine, got dirty, ate fish and bread and drank wine, and healed sick people at a touch with no place to wash his hands afterward, we sometimes tend to lessen his divinity as the I Am That I Am. Indeed, many people have simply emptied Jesus of divinity altogether, writing him off as either a mythological being or simply a good-hearted fellow who had the misfortune of being much misunderstood and eventually killed for it.

What we can't escape, however, is that Jesus declared himself to be none other than God. This places us at a hard point. The only alternatives, as C. S. Lewis so succinctly said in *Mere Christianity,* are to call him a raving lunatic or to bow down and worship him as Lord. There is no room for nonsensical talk about him being a "really good man," or a "humble teacher" and nothing more than that.

Some call him *Lord*. What does that mean? And what do all the other descriptions and names for Jesus that appear in Scripture mean? Somebody told me that there are more than seven hundred different names for Jesus in the Bible. I wouldn't know. I've never counted. I do know that his names aren't just smuggled by, like some sort of special Scriptural code. They mean something; they bear significance.

All of those names, however, like a constellation around some distant star, surround the name God gave his Son—*Jesus*. When Gabriel appeared before Mary, the sight must have astonished her. When he spoke his message—"you shall bear a child"—the words must have perplexed her. When Gabriel said the child would be named Jesus, Mary must have begun pondering things in her heart.

The name *Jesus* was, in fact, a perfectly ordinary one in biblical times, especially for such an extraordinary event as Gabriel announced. In the Old Testament, such names as Joshua, Hehoshua, and Heshua are variations. High priests and commoners were called Jesus. In all its variations, the name means "God's salvation," or "God is my help."

Perhaps it was given to children as a reminder. In 1908, my father was left in a small basket at the doorstep of an orphanage. Presumably, as was the case in those days, the couple just could not care for him. But they left a note affixed to his blanket that read: "His name is Oliver Luverne Beebee." When, a few weeks later, my grandparents, John and Matilda Timmerman, visited the orphanage, little Oliver was a sickly, weak child. But he was the child they wanted. They renamed him John Johnson Timmerman. The middle name is the significant one. Grandfather was saying, "This is John. John's son. He is our child." In somewhat the same way, God said through Gabriel, "This is Jesus, God's Son and God's salvation." In Jesus that salvation appears as fact, as common as ordinary human flesh, as glorious as a miracle of grace.

We fix our eyes on those two natures of Jesus during Advent—God in human form and Jesus as the miracle of grace. All the other names, titles, and figurative descriptions that help us understand the glory of the Savior focus finally on this one man who lived so briefly in Palestine, but who nonetheless, by being at once divine and human, lives forever.

When I read of that life in the Bible, I am struck by how ordinary Jesus' life really was. He never seemed to hurry toward deadlines but took the task given to him each day. Jesus accepted his own sound advice not to worry about tomorrow. Not until his final week on earth, when his ultimate deadline was the cross on Golgotha, do we hear him making specific plans.

He traveled little, occasionally on a donkey, a few times by boat, but mostly on foot. He found plenty to do in the place where he was. He didn't seek crowds; they came to him. He took time for his friends and loved ones. He liked to draw them aside in a quiet place and enjoy the closeness of their company. Nothing seemed more urgent than playing with children.

Finally, he didn't dress to make the "right appearance." He wore the traditional clothes of the common people. The only robe he wore was a network of bloody welts from the Roman soldiers, and the only crown on his head was woven of sharp thorns.

Indeed, Jesus' life was one of quiet drama reaching a climax so unexpected it shook the world.

If it is important for us to fix our eyes on those two natures of Jesus during Advent in order to understand his person and his work, it is also important to do so in understanding ourselves. Perhaps more so during Advent than at any other spiritual season, we begin to feel how discordant our lives can become. Harsh notes attack us, barely alleviated by carols of joy. Too often our days begin in a rip and unravel from there. We need to draw closer to Jesus to order our private lives.

How do we do that? The selected verse for today answers the question. Jesus, "God's Salvation," calls us during this Advent season to the peace and security of his everlasting power.

Isaiah 45:1–3

Thus says the LORD to his anointed, to Cyrus,
  whose right hand I have grasped
to subdue nations before him
  and strip kings of their robes,
to open doors before him—
  and the gates shall not be closed:
I will go before you
  and level the mountains,
I will break in pieces the doors of bronze
  and cut through the bars of iron,
I will give you the treasures of darkness
  and riches hidden in secret places,
so that you may know that it is I, the LORD,
  the God of Israel, who call you by your name.

Prayer

Lord Jesus, you talk to me in these words,
calling me from a world of distractions
to your peace
which surpasses all understanding.
Teach me to listen,
then to hold your words
close in my heart.
Amen.

Second Week in Advent

MASTER OF THE STORM

The western sky was being eaten up by a cloud bank as dark and dismal-looking as peat moss, which in Michigan meant we had about a 2 percent chance of rain. You only get thunderstorms in Michigan when the sky dawns as blue as my mother's delft plates or you have an outdoor wedding planned for the afternoon. The "On Target" weather person had predicted a clear sky, which raised the percentages of rain considerably.

I took the hint when the sun shut down like a candle pinched out and then I was running to the car. Twin jagged lightning bolts snapped north and south like high-energy strobes, and the ground bucked with the roll of thunder. The first drop must have been a four-inch globule, tossed on a nice, sweet curve that hit me in the left eye as I ducked into the car. I reminded myself that rubber tires are insulators. I wondered about steel-belted radials.

All in all, a car isn't a bad vantage point for watching a thunderstorm, and I do like to watch them. This wasn't a mere sponge bath of a dusty earth. It was a full-fledged storm of wind and waves of rain that scrubbed leaves and land. Of course, it would spot up the car that I had washed just yesterday in anticipation of the predicted week of sunny weather. I wash the car whenever we need rain badly.

So I sat and waited and watched.

I had been in a local nature preserve, forty or so acres of wetlands and shrubbery so dense you couldn't spot a raccoon two feet away, even if their tracks were all over the trail. Where the tall trees grow, the undergrowth of shrubbery gives way to a carpet of trillium delighting in the peaty soil. They pitch their tents under a bouquet of white flowers in the spring and make the air as sweet as a walk through cotton candy. What lures me here, however, are two wooden decks hanging out over the swamp ponds, where I can sit undisturbed in the early morning hours. It is one of my favorite writing spots.

I lean back against the bench in the earliest morning light when mist curls all over the face of the pond. My tools are simple: a quart thermos of black coffee (the green, steel Stanley thermos), a stiff-back Mead Cambridge legal pad (yellow paper—easy on the eyes), and the gray Cross rollerball pen I've used for more years than I care to remember.

That was what I came for, until I felt the weight of humidity rise in the air. When I looked up, I saw shadows leaking down through the hickory and oak trees. A wind worked through the upper branches, then cut curious little eddies across the face of the pond. All the ducks had gone into hiding. It was a good clue to move.

A thunderstorm is a fearful and beautiful thing. The incredible power at once terrifies and leaves one breathless with awe. All the scientific discourses in the world fail to touch one heart-pounding moment of the experience. It is not surprising, then, that Scripture so often evokes the majesty and the mystery of experiencing God as the ruler of the storm. He controls. It is, if you will, his show.

When my own life begs for peace and quiet, I want to remember that. In Psalm 18, David experienced the feeling also. He had called out to God from a pit of distress, and, in his poetic imagination, David sees God as master of the storm. David's descriptions of God's presence evoke the most powerful storm imaginable: "Then the earth reeled and rocked; / the foundations also of the mountains trembled / and quaked, because he was angry" (v. 7). Fire blasts out of the black clouds, bolts of lightning pour over the earth. But all the time, David asserts, God is in absolute control. In fact, "he came swiftly upon the wings of the wind" (v. 10) that bucked the trees and shook the clouds.

Why did God do this? A cynic might say, "Because he could." But that isn't right. God is never revealed as some cosmic power broker, having a good fling with the heavens. He is forever and always a God of design and purpose. His purpose in this case, as David testifies, is to meet David's need.

The Storm Rider came to David's aid, lifting him from his distress and the persecution of the enemies. In David's poem, his enemies are very much like the storm—suffocating him with the winds of power. What the enemies don't know is that the Storm Rider controls the storm, and he can deliver his loved ones from it.

David is delivered, as he says, "out into a broad place" (v. 19). But he wouldn't have known the spaciousness and peace of that place, and the power of God's hand to deliver him, had it not been for the storm. Truly we long to avoid the stormy places in our lives. Nonetheless, our Deliverer, the Storm Rider, still soars on the wings of the wind, holding all things in his control.

Often the Advent season begins for us with a storm rather than spacious peace. On the one hand, our hearts earnestly desire to draw closer to the Savior. In a sense, we would like to crawl into the stable. Maybe there's a corner there where we can sit, just out of the way, but still able to take in all the quiet glory.

The reality, however, sometimes seems like thunderclaps buffeting us. Instead of the stable, malls squeeze us in throngs and squeeze our pocketbooks in the process. Quiet glory disappears under gaudy tinsel. The storm moves inward, conflicting our hearts in waves.

Then we also look to the Storm Rider. I think of another storm he rode, recorded in Mark 4:35–41. In the last light of evening Jesus and his disciples set out to cross the Sea of Galilee. As the night deepened, a storm slammed across the sea, battering the ship and filling it near the sinking point. Jesus, amazingly, was asleep. The frantic disciples awakened him. You can almost picture their faces, some bailing desperately, some beseeching Jesus. You can almost hear them, "Do something!" What they didn't expect was the Storm

Rider. Jesus rose and said to the sea, "Peace! Be still!" (4:39). It was like rebuking a rowdy puppy.

As we set sail into Advent, knowing there will arise some tempestuous seas, we listen for those words. We lock them in our hearts like a treasure. Indeed, it is the greatest treasure of Advent. The Storm Rider steps from his majesty into our very lives, and says, "Peace. Be still."

Mark 4:41

> And they were filled with great awe and said to one another, "Who then is this, that even the wind and the sea obey him?"

Prayer

Lord, quiet the storms—
those I face now
and those that may be coming my way.
While they are huge and fearful
in my life, I know that each
is under your powerful control.
I look to you, my Storm Rider,
to lead me safely through.
Go with me to support me;
go ahead of me to show me your way;
be beneath me to uphold me;
be above me to bless me.
Amen.

Second Monday

UNDER HIS WINGS

Life accelerates and schedules clog. There's always too little time and too much to do. The effects are inevitable. We squeeze things out of our schedules to make time for the relentless "more." We sometimes seem like bees dancing around the garden all day with no hive to return to. Where can I just drop it all?

External storms such as these take their toll. They exact their change from our inner lives. And the toll mounts steadily until, often by surprise, there is just no more reserve left. We are psychologically and spiritually spent. Loneliness and bewilderment leak through us like a thick gray haze. Joy seems suctioned out, leaving echoing hallways of emptiness. The storm has gone inward.

Then we wonder how it happened. How did those once-precious traditions by which we measured God's spirit in us—church attendance, prayer, the sacraments—seem to wither away? At such times, it seems painful just to get out of bed, the tasks of the day impossible. The difficulty with this inward storm, which sucks joy like a whirlwind, is that we try to ride it out ourselves. We wear masks, trying to pretend that everything is all right when in fact everything is all wrong.

We try to ride out the storm ourselves because we have lost touch with the Storm Rider.

This sense of emptiness, loneliness, and joylessness afflicts many believers even in this most joyful of all the liturgical seasons. It should be different, we think, for believers during Advent, but only if we are willing to admit our humanity and our need. Inner thunderstorms are less visible than external ones, but no less terrifying for those experiencing them.

That nature preserve that I visit links with a series of ponds and underground streams that form a wetlands area. In particular, two large ponds, several hundred yards apart, rise from the system. One is secluded and heavily sheltered by willows that brush the water with their gentle fingers and create natural coves for wildlife. Blue herons swoop in and out; hawks and owls hide in the upper branches. The other pond, much larger, lies unguarded in the sun like a flat green mirror. You can study the sky in its glassy sheen.

I sometimes wonder what these two ponds hide beneath their surfaces. Is the bottom smooth and clean? Is it pocked with rusted junk metal? Do any of those nonbiodegradable plastic cups lie trapped in the sediment, lying there year after year without hope of renewal? I don't know. I only see the smooth surface that reflects the beauty of the sky overhead, that ripples silver under moonlight, that turns brassy gold when the sun beats on it.

I am curious about hidden things. I grew up near the shore of Lake Michigan. After a storm, particularly in late summer or early autumn, I still love to walk along the beach. The big waves roll in, shooting foam far up onto the sand. And all the detritus caught behind the sandbars follows. Driftwood lies everywhere, even huge pieces of timber or hewn wood. Bottles, half-filled with sand, sparkle on the beach, and then there are the ugly things—the plastics, the metals, even the garbage—dumped far offshore. The storm has scoured things clean.

Inner storms are something like these two examples. Sometimes we hide all the harsh and broken parts under an apparently calm surface. Sometimes a storm finally cracks the surface and stirs up all that junk. Is there any solution? Any resolution?

During Advent, we are looking at the solution head on. Jesus is the Immanuel—the Lord with us. No problem or pressure is so great that he can't control and quiet it. He knows the deepest, most intimate secrets of our lives, even those like the junk at the depths of a pond or a stormy lake. He alone can cleanse it, pulling out those jagged pieces, even those things, like nonbiodegradable plastic, that just seem never to go away.

If, as we saw in the previous day, it is necessary to give our external storms over to the Storm Rider, it is equally necessary to release our inner storms to him. The Lord, King David said, soars "swiftly upon the wings of the wind." The important thing for us is that those wings, David's figure of speech for God's amazing and absolute power, cover us while they soar the storms. But they also sweep, with no less power, into the lonely and hidden places in our lives. With them comes a feathered whisper of hope: Peace. Be still.

Psalm 73:23–25

Nevertheless I am continually with you;
  you hold my right hand.
You guide me with your counsel,
  and afterward you will receive me with honor.
Whom have I in heaven but you?
  And there is nothing on earth that I desire
    other than you.

Prayer

There are times when my heart trembles, Lord,
as fragile as the leaves under the rustling wind
or as dry grass in an unmown field.
I am fearful then—when the storm moves inward.
Protect me in your perfect peace
each day of my life, I pray.
Amen.

Second Tuesday

Within His Care

Imagine a God who soars on the wings of the wind. Those same winds that toss us around are his playground. He rules the wind. This image also reveals God's profound tenderness toward us. If the storms batter us, God fixes his wings between us and the storm. He gathers us close in a safe place.

The descriptions of God protecting us with his wings, or exercising control over the storms, are so prominent in the Old Testament that the concept must have been deeply ingrained in the Israelite mind. Several instances stand out.

During the construction of the Temple, recorded in the First Book of Kings, the work moved steadily inward, each stage increasing in holiness. The further inward one went, the closer one approached the Ark of the Covenant—representing the very presence of God. The Ark reposed in an inner sanctuary, fully covered with gold, that was 30 feet by 30 feet and 30 feet high—a perfect cube. Here golden cherubim, or representations of angelic powers, hung from the ceiling, their wingtips touching in the center of the room, then stretching out to either side. When one entered that sacred place, one entered under the spread wings of God's angels. This symbolized to the Israelites that God was present, that God protected his people, and that God lovingly drew his people into himself.

The ornate and powerful symbolism of Solomon's Temple testifies that we have a safe place to go under God's wings. But wait a minute, we might say. The temple has now been replaced by the parish church, and sometimes that is the last place I feel safe. I feel exposed, weak, and wounded. Surrounded by all those "normal" people, even by the gaiety of candles and wreaths, I feel like running away rather than drawing near. Sometimes even the Christmas carols seem to mock me.

The image of safety within God's wings didn't stop with Solomon's Temple, however. We don't (can't) earn our place before him, and no honor bestowed on us permits our presence. We have to be nothing other than who we are, and we have to do nothing more than breathe a prayer. Several examples from the Old Testament, where this figurative language arises in anticipation of Jesus' Advent, amply support this truth.

Basically two kinds of figurative wings are ascribed to God in the Old Testament. The eagle's wings seem more like the Storm Rider as they indicate God's special power and care for his people. For example, Exodus records Moses' climb up Mount Sinai to talk with God. Among God's very first words are these: "You have seen what I did to the Egyptians, and how I bore you on eagles' wings and brought you to myself" (19:4). The eagle was the most powerful bird in the Mid-Eastern skies in those days, and a creature of awesome beauty. In this figure of the eagle's wings, God testifies both to his power and to his care. In effect, he translates himself into terms the people can understand. God's power may be inconceivable to us, but we do understand the power of an eagle.

If the first "kind" of wing imagery represents power and care, like the picture in Isaiah 40 of God's downtrodden people being able to soar on "wings like eagles," the second imagery represents God's miraculous presence and loving kindness. By his power he draws us under his wings; by his love he keeps us close. The proper word to use here is that he *cuddles* us under his wings, holding us close. I think back to when my wife or I used to read bedtime stories to the children. They didn't want to sit prim and proper. They wanted an arm around them so they could cuddle close until their eyelids grew heavy. That's the second kind of wings we find representing God.

David, who glimpsed the wings of God's power, also drew immense comfort in the wings of God's tenderness. Like a little child, he pleads in Psalm 17, "…hide me in the shadow of your wings" (v. 8). Things outside there frighten me. Hold me real close. For David, those wings of God were a constant refuge (see Psalm 36:7). In one of his most powerful psalms, the longing seems to erupt from his heart: "Let me abide in your tent forever, / find refuge under the shelter of your wings" (61:4). Again the figure suggests a frightened child running to a parent's side, crying for comfort. The remarkable thing in David's testimony is that the comfort is always there for God's children. We can, in a sense, cuddle up to him within the protective shelter of his wings. We have found a safe place.

Isaiah 40:31

…[B]ut those who wait for the LORD
shall renew their strength,
they shall mount up with wings like eagles,
they shall run and not be weary,
they shall walk and not faint.

Prayer

I confess it, Lord.
Truly there are times that
I would like to be a little child again,
to have a safe place to go to,
free from care and worry.
How I thank you
for being that safe place for me,
sheltering me to your side under your outstretched wings.
Amen.

Second Wednesday

To His Side

We face an important question. How do these Old Testament descriptions of God the Father possibly enter our experience of Advent? What does the figure of the Storm Rider soaring on the wings of the wind have to say about our Advent expectation? How do the wings of the Comforter come to bear upon Jesus? They are good questions and demand two answers.

First, the miracle that Christianity claims for Advent is that Jesus, who is wholly divine and one with the Father in the mystery of the Triune God, is also born fully human. Therefore, every attribute ascribed to God Almighty holds not one degree less for his divine Son. Second, Christians also ground their faith in the fact that Scripture, our revelation of God, is a seamless whole, both Old and New Testaments. They are not separate or two-tiered documents. Every revelation in the Old Testament points toward the New; every act of the New in some way fulfills the Old. Both hold equal and authoritative power in the lives of Christians.

Consider that second important point like this. Say that I am studying a textbook in an animal biology class. Chapter 1 might describe the characteristics—mating habits, food preference, and other distinguishing traits—of a certain species. Chapter 2 describes the weight, the musculature, the definition by appearance of that species. Chapter 3 describes the habitat, whether the prairie of Kansas or forest of New Hampshire, lifestyle—burrowing underground or living in trees—and other such characteristics of how the species lives in its region. But all three chapters are on or about the same species. I have merely acquired different sets of information about it. In much the same way, Scripture may be seen as a cohesive, whole set of chapters (books) about Jesus. Every page points toward Advent—the Immanuel, God with us. It is fully reasonable, therefore, to consider the ways in which the Old Testament descriptions of God—those figures of speech that place his divine mystery in terms we humans can comprehend—apply as fully to Jesus.

For example, we observed in an earlier meditation how the figure of the Storm Rider applies to Jesus. Just as the storms that batter the land or that bring relief to drought are under God's divine control, so too Jesus controlled the tempest on the Sea of Galilee. As the first chapter of John testifies, moreover, Jesus was there at Creation, working with the Father and the Holy Spirit to shape this world we call home. The Maker, moreover, always exercises authority over what is made. We can't forget that we are also his creation, and he has the power and authority to gentle the external and internal storms of our personal life.

But I think it is particularly helpful to see the figure of God's wings as comfort in the life and work of Jesus. When Moses climbed Sinai to speak with God, the earth shook, lightning boiled, and thick clouds stormed across the mountain. It is a fearful thing to come face to face with the living God. We dare not forget, however, that Jesus is also the living God. In Advent we are looking to come face to face with him.

Here is God enfleshed. Do we turn and run? Fall down and hide our faces? Or enter his loving embrace? These are not just questions for the end of time, when Jesus will return to judge the living and the dead, when every knee shall bow and every tongue confess that Jesus is Lord. They are questions we ask right here, right now.

Wonderfully, Jesus has already told us how to look for him, and what to look for. One of the last of the Old Testament prophets, Malachi, who wrote approximately four hundred years before Jesus' birth, had a vision of "The Day of the Lord." The theme is not unusual. That's what prophets do, after all. But the beauty of Malachi's vision is that he sees that "the sun of righteousness shall rise with healing in its wings" (4:2). We're a step beyond power and authority and comfort now. Here we have the reason for them: the healing of God's people. Indeed, that very healing formed the purpose of Jesus' coming into our world at all. He is the healing of the nations embodied.

Don't restrict this healing to Jesus' acts of physical healing. When John sent his messenger to ask Jesus if he was indeed the Christ, Jesus told the messenger to tell John what is seen and heard. He then lists the miracles of healing he has wrought—the blind see, the lame walk, and so forth. This part of Jesus' work on earth reveals his authority as Lord over life and death. By no means do we limit that power, then or now.

Jesus' healing of physical sickness may almost be seen as a metaphor for his greater healing of our spiritual sickness. Someday every human body, healed of a disease or not, will die. But those spiritually healed by Jesus, in the greatest paradox of all history, will live forever. When Malachi speaks of the sun of righteousness with healing in its wings, the words don't refer strictly to a physical body, nor in fact solely to the nation of Israel. They refer to a new life altogether, one beyond the physical torments of this life. Jesus' great healing is eternal life. His dying healed us for all eternity.

Notice the fierce tenderness of this healing. From the figures of eagles and cherubim in the Old Testament, with the Advent of Jesus we suddenly have this beautiful figure: "Jerusalem, Jerusalem, the city that kills the prophets and stones those who are sent to it! How often have I desired to gather your children together as a hen gathers her brood under her wings" (Matthew 23:37). The hen gathers the chicks to protect them. Under her wings they are safe. But most important, she is willing to sacrifice herself for her children.

Jesus spoke these words only days before he was crucified. He then offered himself as the sacrifice for his children. Indeed, we might think of this verse during Easter season, but it is wholly fitting to consider it during Advent also. Look at it like this. During Advent Jesus comes to us, wings spread wide, and he asks us, "Won't you come to me? Here there is protection, comfort, and healing. But above all, life with me eternally."

Matthew 11:28

"Come to me, all you that are weary and are carrying heavy burdens, and I will give you rest."

Prayer

It is good to have quiet, Lord.
Let it settle around me and within me,
by the grace of your Holy Spirit.
Give me pause to find
the healing of your wings,
the tender comfort that can
still all the world's harsh din.
Then, in that blessing of quiet,
use it to draw me safely to your side
where my fears may forever be stilled.
Amen.

Second Thursday

THAT HIDEOUS STRENGTH

The title comes from the third novel in C. S. Lewis' famous Space Trilogy. It concludes a battle between God's work and Satan's power that began in heaven and now has moved to earth. Satan's power has infected earthly institutions—once honorable—with a deadly malignancy. Universities, the media, science, and others have succumbed. The novel, first published in 1946, seems to describe our present age with uncanny insight. At one point in the novel, Ransom, who has been God's instrument in the struggle in the previous novels, says, "You might go East so far that East becomes West and you returned to Britain across the great ocean, but even so you would not have come out anywhere into the light. The shadow of one dark wing is over all Tellus [earth]" (*That Hideous Strength.* New York: Macmillan, 1965, p. 293). The hideous strength in that dark wing seeks humanity as its prey.

I lost sleep the first time I read that novel. It still gives me chills to imagine the dark wings of Satan blotting out the earth while his claws scrabble his prey to his scaly chest. Lewis captures a truly monstrous evil.

Perhaps Satan's most clever design has been to make people less fearful of him. We pretend that somewhere in history he just sort of slipped out of the cosmic picture. We forget that it is the very nature of Satan to appear as an angel of light, to bear sweet and sugary words, and to deceive us in a net of lies. If the net were stripped away, we would see the dark wings and cringe at the horror.

The power of evil has not diminished one iota in our time. It lays hold of the unsuspecting and sucks them up like an appetizer. The reality of evil makes all the more powerful God's revelation to us in his wings of power, protection, comfort, and healing. As we see the darkness invading, however, we look to another powerful description of God. This figure describes Jesus' power to blast the power of darkness, shred the net of lies, rock Satan back on his heels, and ultimately bind him in the Lake of Fire. For a light has come into the darkness.

A series of light images come together in Scripture, many of them pointing toward Advent. We symbolize this by the sequence of candles in the Advent wreath, lighting one each Sunday until Christmas when the Christ candle is lit. The sequence suggests the same thing as the Scriptural descriptions. Coming out of the darkness, overwhelming the darkness, is a light for the ages.

The very first act of God recorded in Scripture, in fact, was the creation of light. Genesis 1:2 tells us that the earth was "a formless void," that "darkness covered the face of the deep." Here already we find the vast, empty expanse of darkness. No life can grow there. Darkness sucks all things inward; it never grants life. Imagine the emptiness, the desolate lifelessness of this space clad in darkness.

Then in one majestic proclamation, God makes his first creative act on this earth. It is by his word only. No special hocus-pocus needed. God said, "Let there be light," and over the entire face of this globe light began to move like a living thing itself. Earth was now, and only now, ready for life. At a word, God made a division, separating light from darkness, preparing the way for night and day. Trying to visualize all this in my mind's eye makes me a bit dizzy. Even if I can't contain it in my limited imagination, this point becomes clear to my mind—God is in absolute, undeniable control of the light over darkness.

Another example of God's authority over physical light and darkness comes to mind. Joshua had forged aggressively into the Promised Land, taking one by one the territories God appointed for the Israelites. The five kings of the Amorites thought they would outfox Joshua by marching to Gibeon and making their stand there in a great force. When a messenger alerted Joshua of the scheme, he marched all night to Gibeon and launched a surprise attack. The Amorite armies he fought were massive, and he was on a mission to destroy them utterly. He prayed that the Lord would halt the motion of the sun and the moon, right where they were in the middle of the sky. And God did. For a full day the sun and moon stood still (see Joshua 10).

For Joshua, the sun stood still at its noontime zenith. There was no dark place for the enemies to run to and hide. But we think of a third time when God intervened with the natural physics of light. This was also at noontime, but the light disappeared.

At high noon, when three men were nailed to crosses on Golgotha, "darkness came over the whole land until three in the afternoon" (Luke 23:44). From 12 until 3, the hours of Jesus' dying. What was the Father saying? Could those legions of angels Jesus could have called upon not bear to watch their Lord die? Did the darkness ooze out of the evil in the land that put the Prince of Peace on the cross? We don't know, but it was as dark and fearful as only death can be.

This is part of the reality of Advent. A darkness lies ahead. But the light, not just the one created by God but the one that is in fact *God*, is far greater. Even past the darkness, then, we see a light. During the following days of meditations, we will explore the powerful and glorious figures of light that help us know Jesus.

Luke 24:6–8

> "Remember how he told you, while he was still in Galilee, that the Son of Man must be handed over to sinners, and be crucified, and on the third day rise again." Then they remembered his words.

Prayer

Lord, I pray that I may find great comfort
in your power of light. On a day
when sunlight pours over early snow
that glistens like billions of diamonds,
or a day gray with rain and lowering clouds,
may I find you, the Giver of Light,
in all places at all times.
Amen.

Second Friday

"THE BATTLE IS MINE"

Charles Williams, an English novelist and friend of C. S. Lewis, wrote a strange, haunting novel called *War in Heaven.* We have little doubt, as Saint Paul wrote, that a battle between powers and principalities rages daily (see Ephesians 6:12). As seen in the previous two meditations, however, the arena for that warfare does not simply lie "out there" in some far, detached realm. It has moved to earth, sometimes uncomfortably close to our own souls.

I confess that I have misgivings about people who never seem to have a problem in their lives. I think I am more comfortable with those who have walked through the valley. They have faced some human trial that reminded them of their dreadful need for God. Perhaps you know those others I mean, those who never seem to have a problem.

Their house is the neatest on the block; their cars the shiniest. They take frequent vacations and remodel parts of the house each year—having the work done by professionals, of course. Their two children are always neat as photographic models, clad in the latest styles. They are straight A students. Both intend to be neurosurgeons.

Am I just jealous? My rambunctious brood of four kids always had something going to keep me off balance. My house's plumbing acts up often, the underground sprinkling quit working long ago, the gardens grow weeds with abandon. Maybe I am jealous of those who flirt with perfection.

But I also know that under that apparent perfection, many people struggle mightily with events, thoughts, and desires that they would never expose to the light of day. Or to the Light of God's grace.

I sometimes think a mark of the strength of our Christian faith is not how carefully we work to appear perfect but how willing we are to admit our need.

The fact is that Advent does *not* mean much of anything unless there is a need for it. Either the hideous strength shadows both our world and personal lives and we desperately need the light of our Advent Savior, or all is well with the world and Satan is a myth—in which case, the Advent Savior is a cosmic hoax. There are no other ways to have it.

And that is precisely how Scripture has it. The Bible is a testament of people looking for the light; it is also a testament of how the light is found.

God's people in the Bible were not altogether unlike us. They dressed differently, ate some other foods, looked a bit different—that's really about it. The essentials are the same. Every one of them was a sinner standing in the need of grace. But to every one of them the promise of grace was also extended. As so often happens in Scripture, that grace is figured in physical or imaginative ways.

When the Israelites fled Egypt, they knew God's grace was with them in a very tangible way: "The LORD went in front of them in a pillar of cloud by day, to lead them along the way, and in a pillar of fire by night, to give them light, so that they might travel by day and by night" (Exodus 13:21). I would guess that at first that pillar of fire must have been terrifying—this is the power of the Lord! But surely its light also brought comfort—our Lord is guiding us! Because no mere shape can contain him, God repeatedly manifests himself in fire. We think of the burning bush before Moses and his sudden awareness that he was on sacred ground. Or we think of the waves of fire and lightning that rocked Mount Sinai when Moses spoke with God to receive the law.

Fire is the source of comfort and peace, but also the devouring power. Its light reveals us as we are; its energy refines our lives as if we were dipped in a crucible.

In the Old Testament these images of God as a Lord of fire appear often. His wrath descended like fire to devour his enemies (see Psalm 18:8). Literal fire fell from heaven to burn an altar (see 2 Kings 1:10). God's people built altar fires to make "a pleasing odor" to God (see Leviticus 3:5).

Fire also appears in another way, however. In this case, we have to remember a physical reality of daily living for the Israelites. We are accustomed to the casual use of electricity—indeed, in our time of environmental concern, we sometimes wish there were less of it. The Israelites knew light in only two ways. One of course was the light of the sun and the moon, and many families were entirely restricted to that source. The other light came from obviously more expensive sources of wood fires or oil lamps. One just did not make a fire casually, or light a lamp for no reason at all. Light was not plentiful; that little amount was cherished and protected. When the shepherds in the field saw the light of the angels dancing in the sky, it must have struck them as an extravaganza beyond all measure—a riot of light. What could call for this…this profligacy of light?

So it is that literal fire, so often associated with God in Scripture, carried the multilayered forces of power, authority, direction, and comfort. The light itself was held as something precious, almost miraculous in its presence.

But there can't be light without fire—not without this precious energy.

To my mind, one of the most precious and powerful names Jesus uses for himself appears in John 8:12, the so-called Gospel of Light. Surrounded by the badgering Pharisees, Jesus said: "I am the light of the world. Whoever follows me will never walk in darkness but will have the light of life." That name links the New Testament with the Old, and Jesus with the Father, like a padlock on a chain. Here, now, is the light of the Father's fiery glory, dwelling on this earth to lead us out of darkness into the light of life.

1 Peter 2:9

> But you are a chosen race, a royal priesthood, a holy nation, God's own people, in order that you may proclaim the mighty acts of him who called you out of darkness into his marvelous light.

Prayer

In a season of lights,
I pray I will not be blinded
to the true light. May your light,
Jesus, flood me so powerfully
that everything else dims
by comparison.
Amen.

Second Saturday

ILLUMINATION

We sometimes find ourselves trying to balance our lives somewhere between gray and white, a delicate dance in the shadows. We might wonder when the Lord of Light will simply sweep the gray away.

Several years ago I spent a few days on Nantucket Island, just a short hop by plane from the mainland over the Atlantic. The quaint village crowds between the harbor hills, following crooked streets around sharp corners. It is a famous place, of course, and I was glad to spend a few days here—glad too that as a guest speaker at a conference I was not paying my own way. The harbor was once the busiest whaling port on the eastern coast. Here Melville wrote much of *Moby Dick,* and here Steinbeck wrote much of *East of Eden.* Here also the fog can sock in for days on end. It is no accident that people call Nantucket Island "The Gray Lady."

During free time on my second day there, I toured the island's oceanography lab. When I stepped outside the dank, dripping corridors of the lab, it seemed nothing had changed. The fog was thick and clammy. An elderly man walking out behind me said to no one in particular, "Yep. Pretty hard to believe the sun's up there shining away with all this fog around."

On my final morning on the island the sun burned through the fog with dawn's first rays. I walked far down the shore, well beyond the harbor. The light played above the green sea like speckled beans floating. Against a weathered post, driven in once as a beacon or a property marker perhaps, a large conch shell lay half-hidden in the sand. With a brush of stiff sand grass, I cleaned away the damp sand inside its chambers. It grew lighter by the moment, as if rising heavenward. Its porcelain valves, nearly translucent against the eastern dawn, seemed to spiral directly toward the sun.

For a moment I wondered if I could pack it carefully enough to take it home. But it seemed more fitting here. I positioned it carefully upon the post, where it leaned in the sea breeze between heaven and earth.

In a way, we are all so positioned. Freed from the wet sand that holds us down, Someone has lifted us, cleaned all the clogged spaces, and helped us rise toward the morning light.

Jesus names himself as the "Light of the World" (John 8:12). That name calls forth a host of expectations and years of yearning from the Old Testament. In a sense, we can picture the people and prophets walking constantly in a thin fog. But they believed the sun would shine, that a power higher and holier and mightier than the fog that draped down close to the surface of their lives would break through.

In tracing the Old and New Testament references to light, several large patterns appear. I call them "outer" and "inner." In the outer pattern, we see that the God of Light holds power over the darkness of this world, just as the sun has the power to burn away the fog that blankets the land. He is the Creator of light, a gift he graciously bestowed. Second, the light also illuminates our hearts and minds and kindles our awareness of Jesus' presence in our lives. We need the light of grace to help us see clearly.

The first, the exterior illumination or the power of God that holds sway over evil and darkness, is amply attested. We have already considered several such references. When David testifies that "The LORD is my light and my salvation; / whom shall I fear?" (Psalm 27:1), he clearly celebrates the Lord who has empowered him in battle and his kingly role. Similar examples are numerous—God is the protective and delivering light against evil.

The second pattern of light is far more personal. It speaks to our deepest need. When the battle turns inward to the human spirit, when all our hopes seem clouded behind a dense, gray fog bank in the mind, we long for the cleansing power of interior illumination. We need the fierce intimacy of Jesus' presence. More than sets of doctrinal knowledge, more than glorious deeds, more than all the homilies in the world, we need the light of the Savior renewing the dark places within us. Of these moments Scripture, with its terrifying realism, is also deeply mindful.

Psalm 13 records such a moment in the life of our warrior-king David. Whatever the conquests and glory God had given him, David feels brutally, hopelessly, forgotten by God. "How long will you hide your face from me?" he cries. In verse 3 he shapes his prayer like this: "Consider and answer me, O LORD my God! / Give light to my eyes, or I will sleep the sleep of death." "Light to [the] eyes" was a common prayer for restoration, but it speaks more specifically to an interior illumination—a "seeing" that God is at hand.

These two powerful patterns are like hands that hold us in hope during Advent. They also, as we see tomorrow in the lives of several of the great prophets, nurture our expectations for the coming King.

2 Corinthians 4:6

> For it is the God who said, "Let light shine out of darkness," who has shone in our hearts to give the light of the knowledge of the glory of God in the face of Jesus Christ.

Prayer

Lord, sometimes I wonder what I carry
in this jar of clay to be worthy
in the light of your grace.
I realize it is nothing I can bring,
but only the light of the knowledge
of your boundless grace
that has won the victory over my own darkness.
To God be the glory.
Amen.

Third Week in Advent

GREAT EXPECTATION

As a boy I was one of those who waited with heart-pounding anticipation for Christmas morning. I waited for presents.

I grew up in one of those big old houses that seemed to ramble all over the place. On the second-floor back addition was a huge, three-season bedroom. It was mine, all nine windows and seemingly acres of space to hold a litter of books, puzzles, models, and other boy stuff. Truly I loved that room. The only problem was that by mid-October not a furnace in the world could keep up with the drafts creeping through those nine windows. Then I had to move to a hot, cramped little room at the foot of the attic stairs.

The "big room," as we then called it, served a new seasonal purpose. By late October the first Christmas packages would start to appear. By late November there was a pile of bright-colored packages. We didn't worry that in a family of four kids most of them held things like shirts, socks, even underwear. The packages were what mattered. And some of them would hold toys—model cars or puzzles or books.

When the house was silent I would sneak like a culprit into the big room, intent on finding which packages held the clothes and which the "good stuff." I counted the packages to see how I was doing compared with the others. This could go two ways. Fewer packages could mean I was either getting something really neat, or say, just a sweater or so. Sometimes I was even in there long enough to lift a corner of wrapping paper and try to peek inside. Then my mother, blessed with the keenest ears on earth or simply knowing her oldest son too well, would call from downstairs, "Timmy, you're not in the big room, are you?" I'd slither out quickly, shut the door quietly, and call back, "No, Mom." Well, I wasn't at that moment.

So the days generated a pure electrical current of anticipation in me. On Christmas morning I awakened in the middle of the night. I stayed in bed as long as I could. Along about 5 AM I moved all the presents down to the living room (my job by right of age) and stacked them by the chairs where we normally sit in our Christmas circle. I could hardly stand it! By 5:30 I asked my parents' permission to awaken the others, and, interpreting their groggy groans as a "yes," started shouting into the other bedrooms.

As a boy, I had a pretty strong hope and certain expectation that Christmas was actually coming. First, I had evidence from past experience. Second, I had that growing pile of presents in the big room. Third, I saw the days of the calendar pass by toward that magic morning. But what if it had never happened before? Or if there were no calendar? No firm expectation that it might happen in my lifetime? All I had was belief, a promise, and courage?

Such was the case of the Old Testament prophets when they spoke of the light to come. Their anticipation was every inch as high as mine, their belief rock-steady, their courage unmatchable. Their calendar differed slightly. The event they foresaw would happen in God's divine moment. Yet they expected the great gift as if it were there to unwrap tomorrow.

No prophet's voice announced this expectation more powerfully than Isaiah. In the great "Advent chapter" of Isaiah 9, the prophet proclaims in the first two verses:

The people who walked in darkness
have seen a great light;
those who lived in a land of deep darkness—
on them light has shined.

The light is so real to Isaiah that it is already present, a truth from God. Then he proclaims, and I can feel the excitement in his words, "For a child has been born for us, / a son given to us" (v. 6). Yet, the words seem fearfully odd, as he goes on to say that this child will be the "...Mighty God." God himself! Born to us. Now there's an event worth looking for.

What do we do while we wait, Isaiah? What keeps the expectation fresh and forceful in us? Isaiah answers for God in verse 6 of chapter 49, "I will give you as a light to the nations, / that my salvation may reach to the end of the earth." Waiting expectantly is not just a matter of sitting on our hands, then. We have to prepare; we have to give our knowledge of salvation in bright packages of love to others. Let them feel the anticipation, peer under the wrappings. This is precisely the thrust of Isaiah's words in chapter 60, verses 1–3:

Arise, shine; for your light has come,
and the glory of the LORD has risen upon you.
For darkness shall cover the earth,
and thick darkness the peoples;
but the LORD will arise upon you,
and his glory will appear over you.
Nations shall come to your light,
and kings to the brightness of your dawn.

Our great and extraordinary expectations are, as Isaiah says, already fulfilled, unwrapped, and ready to be put to use by us.

Our light has come. Our Advent gift to others is to let our light shine into their lives.

Luke 11:33

"No one after lighting a lamp puts it in a cellar, but on the lampstand so that those who enter may see the light."

Prayer

This season unfurls its bright banners.
The lights dazzle, sometimes searing my eyes.
I pray for the ability to see clearly
the true light in the expectation of Advent.
Then, by your grace, Lord,
may I set it out, on a stand,
for others to see it in me.
Amen.

Third Monday

BRIGHT MORNING STAR

Isaiah began his prophetic ministry in the year 740 BC, long before Jesus—the light that he prophesied—was born. Looking at the numbers on paper, we don't feel particularly overwhelmed. We live in an age of large numbers, most of which we simply can't comprehend. How can the national debt be more than $4 trillion? Just what does that mean? How can the richest man in the world be worth $54 billion, at this writing? How do we measure that against our incomes or our budgets?

Seven-hundred and fifty doesn't seem like that much with such numbers. But these were years, not dollars, and that changes our whole way of looking at things.

A little more than one hundred fifty years ago the first wagon trains, drawn by oxen, were pulling out of St. Louis on the long journey west. Just a little over one hundred thirty years ago, George Armstrong Custer lost the infamous battle at Little Big Horn. Which of those wagon train pioneers could have predicted that cars and trucks would flash by at seventy miles per hour on concrete roads? Which of the Sioux warriors or the doomed cavalry would have predicted such weaponry as cruise missiles or stealth fighter planes?

And yet, Isaiah has the pure audacity to say that a light is coming to the world, that he would come as a child, and that he would be called "Mighty God."

You see, the darkness in this case is our pure unknowing, our reluctance to believe. Who can shatter that darkness with light, and penetrate our unknowing, but the Bright Morning Star?

The morning star is the powerful one. When the lesser stars have been hazed over by the shifting light of the distant sun, the morning star holds faithful and true. It has blazed throughout the night, but it holds steady in its position as the sun's first rays streak the sky. It is our guide, if you will, from darkness to light. It announces the dawn, almost as if its distant, radiant power is transformed to the sun itself, which brings light to our earth.

The very idea pulses with energy. And to think that centuries before Isaiah saw the light coming in a little child called Mighty God.

Of all the names, titles, and descriptive figures ascribed to Jesus, however glorious and meaningful each may be, the Bright Morning Star is the one that takes my breath away. Amazingly, that prophecy antedates Isaiah. Way back in the book of Numbers (24:17), Balaam prophesied that,

I see him, but not now;
I behold him, but not near—
a star shall come out of Jacob,
and a scepter shall rise out of Israel.

In his vision, Balaam sees the coming one, but he is not here, not yet. He will come, as did Jesus, like a star out of the lineage of Jacob. His scepter will be his rule and his divinity to deliver his people from the bondage of darkness.

Now here arrives a beautiful parallel. Remember those shepherds encamped in the fields when Jesus was born? At that same moment, a supernatural brightness of angels shattered the darkness and startled them awake with singing. And at the same time, a star of enormous brilliance appeared to Magi in the east, leading them on their months-long journey to Jerusalem. These Magi, who were a priestly royalty in their native Persia, immediately apprehended that the star signified One of eternal royalty. They came, as Matthew tells us, only to worship.

The prophets looked ahead, with that uncanny vision given by God. The shepherds and Magi celebrated the glory of the unveiling. The moment came. But how do we look back on the moment with reflective hearts? Do we leave the Morning Star out there hanging in some historical heavens? The apostle Peter gives us the answer.

In his two letters the once thunderous, hot-tempered, and quick-to-act Peter writes as a deeply thoughtful and loving person. Well, he had been through a few things, hadn't he? Not the least of which was the love of God for a sinner and a traitor. Perhaps that accounts for the gentleness of his words. Toward the last years of his life he wrote his second letter, a deeply moving work of wisdom and encouragement. We can do worse than look to Peter for answers.

In the Second Book of Peter, the apostle warns us that, even though the light has come, much of the world will persist in darkness. False teachers will edge their way into the church. Satan will twist the truth until it seems like barbed wire. Peter assures us, however, that we can escape the prevailing darkness by clinging to the divine power of Jesus (see 2 Peter 1:3–4). But more than this, we have the power to change the darkness, for the light of the Bright Morning Star now lives within us: "So we have the prophetic message more fully confirmed. You will do well to be attentive to this as to a lamp shining in a dark place, until the day dawns and the morning star rises in your hearts" (1:19). Truly, that Morning Star already rises in our hearts, whenever we locate and fight against the darkness.

But that isn't the end of the story, for Peter's comment is also prophetic. A day will come when the Morning Star will rise again, when all darkness will be rolled up and cast aside, when those with the Morning Star already in their hearts will dance for joy. Jesus himself gives these promises: "It is I, Jesus, who sent my angel to you with this testimony for the churches. I am the root and the descendant of David, the bright morning star" (Revelation 22:16).

Revelation 22:20

The one who testifies to these things says, "Surely I am coming soon."

Amen. Come, Lord Jesus!

Prayer

Until that day, Lord Jesus,
lift up the light of your countenance upon us,
cause your face to shine upon us,
and give to us, and to all those we love,
your peace.
Amen.

Third Tuesday

ARISE, SHINE

Let's spend a few minutes yet with Isaiah, that great prophet of the Messiah. Isaiah stood physically in time approximately seven hundred years before Jesus was born. In his spiritual vision—his prophecy—he stands at the time when Jesus is born. He operates in God's time then, as God opens a window on things to be. When Isaiah sees these things, he reports them to his people in terms they can understand.

Toward the end of his majestic prophecy, Isaiah almost seems to wonder if he has made those things revealed to him by God clear to the people. He feels the weight of his prophetic responsibility. He reminds me of a teacher working intently with a student who can't quite grasp the problem, much less the answer. In the very first verse of chapter 53, Isaiah says (with frustration?), "Who has believed what we have heard? / And to whom has the arm of the LORD been revealed?" If you remember, this is the same chapter that details Jesus' redemption for us. He would be "despised and rejected by others" (v. 3). Nevertheless, "by his [wounds] we are healed" (v. 5).

Faced with the difficulty of making his message understood by a people who often suffered a willful hearing loss, Isaiah changes his tone in the final chapters to an excited proclamation of peace. Think of it this way. A few years ago, the "Emmanuel" concert played in our city, and I very much wanted tickets. I waited with some anxiety until the day tickets were released. I wanted four tickets since we wanted to take some friends along, and of course I wanted decent seats. As the publicity mounted, so did my anxiety. It looked like a sellout. When I finally got the tickets, however, I had the peace of knowing I would be there and could enjoy the excitement of looking forward to the event.

As Isaiah looks out over history to a moment to come, he seems to be bursting with excitement himself. In chapter 60 he calls out, "Arise, shine, for your light has come, / and the glory of the LORD has risen upon you" (v. 1).

The Gospel of John helps clarify Isaiah's prophecy for us. There is an old story about a little boy drawing a picture of God. As he worked with it, his mother said, "No one really knows what God looks like." To which the boy responded, "They will when I get through." In a sense, John draws us a picture of Jesus in terms of light. Already in chapter 1 he announces that "in him was life, and the life was the light of all people. The light shines in the darkness, and the darkness did not overcome it" (v. 4–5). It is almost as if John is saying, "Listen. This Jesus is exactly the one Isaiah talked about." Life and light go together since this Light gives life.

In verse 14, John adds "And the Word became flesh and lived among us, and we have seen his glory, the glory as of a father's only son, full of grace and truth." Where was Jesus' glory? The miracle of the Incarnation gives us the answer. The Prophesied One is here. God appeared in human flesh. The unimaginable glory of God is now the Light that illumines our path through life.

This message of Jesus' light threads through John's entire Gospel, weaving it into one beautiful tapestry glowing with grace and truth. John records Jesus' own words to make this perfectly clear. Talking with the Jews at one point, Jesus says, "For just as the Father has life in himself, so he has granted the Son also to have life in himself" (5:26). Jesus is the very embodiment of life. But as the light shines upon others, illuminating their path, so too this life is given for others to lead them into eternal glory with Jesus. Again, we consider Jesus' own words, "This is indeed the will of my Father, that all who see the Son and believe in him may have eternal life; and I will raise them up on the last day" (6:40).

Nonetheless, the time came when everyone thought the light was extinguished. Jesus cautioned about just such a time: "The light is with you for a little longer. Walk while you have the light, so that the darkness may not overtake you. If you walk in the darkness, you do not know where you are going" (John 12:35). And the moment did come. The darkness stormed over Calvary. At noon the sky turned black. An earthquake rattled the earth. What happens when the darkness comes, and the Light of the world flickers out?

But Jesus' promises are true. We can barely understand the edges of them, never quite grasping the whole in this world of shadows. We have to remember that Jesus is the Light and Life. We have to remember his frequent declarations of love and life for his believers. We remember that he promised, "[My] peace I leave with you" (John 14:27). Remember and believe also that death and the grave were shattered by the Light of Everlasting Life on Sunday morning. The light is victorious, and if it was at Jesus' time, so too it is today.

Even that magnificent story of Light and Life isn't the end of the matter, however. Like Isaiah, another John was also given a vision of things far in the future. This John was an elderly man, writing from a Roman penal colony on the island of Patmos. And his vision confirmed Jesus' promise that all who look to the Son will be raised at the last day. Chapter 4 of that great Revelation opens upon the throne of heaven. If we look as John did, "in the spirit," the sight we behold seems too bright to endure. The twenty-four elders are dressed in white with crowns of gold. Lightning flashes around the throne. Before it "burn seven flaming torches" (v. 5). And at the very center of all this bannered light is…a lamb, "standing as if it had been slaughtered" (5:6). Before this lamb—the one prophesied by Isaiah (see 53:7)—all the mighty hosts of heaven bow and raise a thunderous song of glory. Thousands upon thousands of angels encircle the throne to sing praise and honor.

This is the Light everlasting. The Light came into the world, overcame the darkness, and gave us life that we may be with him forever in his glory.

John 14:27

"Peace I leave with you; my peace I give to you. I do not give to you as the world gives. Do not let your hearts be troubled, and do not let them be afraid."

Prayer

Our risen Lord,
our peace lies in knowing beyond any doubt
that you were born in Bethlehem
as the Light and the Life of humanity;
that on Calvary you died to set us free
to see your glory,
and that on the third day
you rose from death.
By doing so, you have assured
our hope that we will be with you
in your glory forever and ever.
Amen.

Third Wednesday

The Son of Man

As we study the names and titles of Jesus in the context of the Advent season, it may sometimes seem that we dance around the edges of truly knowing him. Words only bring us part way. Even analogies—word pictures—only point us in a direction, leaving the final end incomplete. As Paul wrote in 1 Corinthians 13:12, "Now I know only in part; then I will know fully, even as I have been fully known."

I, too, long to know fully. So many questions. What will it be like to meet Jesus face to face? What is God really like? Or what is heaven like?

If I glance back at Paul's words once more, however, I find comfort in them. Why do I, with my limited understanding and experience, feel that I have to know fully? That knowledge would shatter the darkness of my understanding like a strobe light pressed on my eyelids. I study the names of Jesus since this is one way he has chosen to reveal himself. The true comfort in Paul's words is that, here and now, "I am fully known."

This fact is particularly important, I believe, as we study that title "Son of Man," which brings us right to the mysterious heart of the Incarnation.

After a careful study of the New Testament, no one can doubt Jesus' claim to divinity. Among the first to pay homage to him as the Son of God were the demons. In the synagogue at Capernaum, a man possessed by a demon cried out, "Let us alone! What have you to do with us, Jesus of Nazareth? Have you come to destroy us? I know who you are, the Holy One of God" (Luke 4:34). Later, the two Gadarene demoniacs shouted, "What have you to do with us, Son of God?" (Matthew 8:29). And during his temptation in the wilderness, Satan, the father of demons, openly referred to Jesus as the "Son of God" (see Matthew 4:3, 5).

Jesus' divine title as "Son of God" appears several other times. For example, the Holy Spirit announced Jesus' divinity at his baptism (see Luke 3:22). When Jesus walked on the water to Peter, Peter exclaimed, "Truly you are the Son of God" (Matthew 14:33). Jesus himself spoke of doing his Father's will (see John 6:38–40). There can be no question from such passages that Jesus' Father is God himself. That Jesus is the Son of God is the overwhelming theme of other New Testament books as well.

Well it *should* be, for this is the heart of Advent and all Christianity: The Son of God "became flesh and lived among us" (John 1:14). For us, this is an unfathomable truth. Why should one give up the glories of heaven to live as a man and to die like a criminal—worse, to die for crimes not his?

But reverse the perspective. For the Son of God, the truly remarkable thing must have been to become human. Thus, it is not surprising that Jesus names himself over and over as the Son of Man. The title is used more than sixty times in the synoptic Gospels and several times in the Gospel of John. Outside the gospels, which, of course, concern themselves with the life of Jesus, the name is used only a few times. One of those is in the Acts of the Apostles, where Stephen says, "I see the heavens opened and the Son of Man standing at the right hand of God!" (Acts 7:56). Jesus calls himself the Son of Man repeatedly, reinforcing another marvelous truth: the Son of God is fully human.

But why the title "Son of Man?" Precisely because all that Jesus does and all that he means is present in himself, in his bodily form. In fact, Jesus uses the title when he is making some of his greatest claims for himself.

As Son of Man, he is the redeemer: "For the Son of Man came to seek out and to save the lost" (Luke 19:10). And "For the Son of Man came not to be served but to serve, and to give his life a ransom for many" (Mark 10:45).

As Son of Man, he is resurrected from the dead, having paved a way redeemed humans may follow. To Martha, Jesus said, "I am the resurrection and the life. Those who believe in me, even though they die, will live, and everyone who lives and believes in me will never die" (John 11:25–26).

As Son of Man, he has ascended and prepared a place for those who will be resurrected to be with him: "I tell you, From now on you will see the Son of Man seated at the right hand of Power and coming on the clouds of heaven" (Matthew 26:64).

And, finally, as Son of Man, he will return again: "For the Son of Man is to come with his angels in the glory of his Father, and then he will repay everyone for what has been done" (Matthew 16:27).

None of these events is possible unless Jesus became the Son of Man. The true Glory lies here: The Son of God became Son of Man to redeem the lost, to resurrect the redeemed, to ascend and prepare a place in glory, and to return again to judge the world. The celebration of this Advent miracle rocks all the knowledge of this earth because it only happened once. Indeed, it only had to happen once—through the Incarnation of the Son of God as the Son of Man.

Romans 5:17

> If, because of the one man's trespass, death exercised dominion through that one, much more surely will those who receive the abundance of grace and the free gift of righteousness exercise dominion in life through the one man, Jesus Christ.

Prayer

I thank you, Lord,
for leaving the splendor of heaven,
for leaving your throne at the right hand
of God…and for what?
To be born as man in a world
filled with frenzy,
to be led to a cross where you died unjustly,
to be laid in a tomb from which you arose,
and for promising
to return again,
to judge all humankind,
and to take with you all believers
to everlasting life.
Amen.

Third Thursday

MESSIAH: THE PROMISED ONE

In our own Advent calendars we're drawing close now. We're leaning on tiptoe for a look into Bethlehem. Surely we will celebrate at home with family and with friends, but that merely shadows our celebration of Jesus. If these were empty gifts under the tree, if the stockings were empty and the cupboard bare, we still would have the greatest gift ever given. Unwrapping this gift from the pages of the gospels, we find life everlasting, riches untold, forgiveness of sins, release from guilt, grace like a river. We find the Messiah.

But who and what is a Messiah? How does that name *Messiah* enter into the vocabulary of Advent? To begin to understand this, we have to turn back through many pages of history to God's very first "Merry Christmas" to us. Once again, an analogy may help us.

In C. S. Lewis's well-known story, *The Lion, the Witch and the Wardrobe,* four English children find themselves in the fantasy world of Narnia, a land encased in a frigid landscape that has endured a hundred winters without a thaw. The White Witch has placed her spell on the land, enslaving it to a climate as hard and cold as her own cruel nature. The worst thing, however, is that it is always winter and never Christmas. One can imagine the joy of the Narnians when, after a hundred years of unrelenting expectation, Father Christmas finally arrives.

The fantasy world of always winter but never Christmas may

seem quite unlike our own world. With the commercialization of Christmas into an eight- to ten-week sell-a-thon, it almost seems as if it's always Christmas—even before winter arrives. One wearies of seeing the great Advent reduced to mere adventure in toy shops. We wonder, "How much earlier can they make it?" and then each year stand amazed as stores and malls step up the Christmas advertising just a few days earlier. In the race for the dollar, Christmas runs well, even if it is renamed "Happy Holidays" by the national chains.

The analogy helps us focus on God's earliest Christmas, for we find it promised already in the Book of Genesis at the dawn of history.

God's clean, new world was hardly made when sin wriggled into it like a vicious blot. Imagine an artist laboring over a beautiful landscape painting, so full it ripples with life—birds in feathered raiment, fish sparkling in silver waters, animals at play in gardens and forests. When at last the artist finishes, imagine someone cruelly slashing the painting so that the original is irreparably marred. This is but a pale representation of the wound in God's living Creation when sin entered the world.

One might expect God, standing before the blighted ruins of his perfect artistry, to rage against sin. Since he is perfectly just, God must exact retribution. Every sin has its price. But here at the very dawn of time, God responds instead by wishing his people the earliest Merry Christmas. One shall come, he says, who will bear the full terror of the penalty for their sin. In Genesis 3:15, God promises to the temptation-bringing serpent:

> *"I will put enmity between you and the woman,*
> *and between your offspring and hers;*
> *he will strike your head,*
> *and you will strike his heel."*

A future offspring in the lineage of this first woman Eve, a child born to human parents, will somehow crush the serpent's head while bearing the serpent's sting. God looks across the centuries and sees his son, Jesus, on the cross.

Yes, the serpent shall bruise Jesus' heel. The sting of sin, the weight of our stripes, and the burden of our iniquities will be upon him there on the cross. God always keeps his promises. We shouldn't be any more surprised when he reminds us through Isaiah of the coming Messiah. Part of Isaiah's profound vision of the Messiah to come was also a backward-looking vision. Isaiah (53:4–5) reminds the Israelites of God's words:

Surely he has borne our infirmities
and carried our diseases;
yet we accounted him stricken,
struck down by God, and afflicted.
But he was wounded for our transgressions,
crushed for our iniquities;
upon him was the punishment that made us whole,
and by his bruises we are healed.

Our first knowledge of the Messiah, then, is that he is one promised by God. His appearance in human history is part of God's eternal plan for the redemption of human history. While we can't fully understand the mind of God apart from what he has revealed to us, our joy at Advent is that the Promised One has come. That makes all the difference. If this great promise is true, as the Bible testifies from its first pages, then all of God's promises are true.

There in the scarred Eden, when by all rights God's wrath could be kindled, in love and kindness beyond imagination he wishes us the earliest Merry Christmas. The gift of his Son, Jesus, brings our winter of sin to an end.

1 John 4:9–10

> God's love was revealed among us in this way: God sent his only Son into the world so that we might live through him. In this is love, not that we loved God but that he loved us and sent his Son to be the atoning sacrifice for our sins.

Prayer

This indeed is love, Lord:
that Jesus came and dwelt among men.
When the angels sang hallelujah,
glory to the newborn king,
few rejoiced on earth—shepherds,
Wise Men, Joseph and Mary and their relation.
But how that song of rejoicing,
that glorious hallelujah has spread.
My song of praise joins in: Glory, hallelujah
to the newborn king.
Amen.

Third Friday

THE BRANCH

With all the preparation and celebration of this season, we need to pause and ask a very important question: "Just who did the Old Testament prophets expect?" What would he do? How would he work in the world—as King? As Prophet? As a commoner? These questions help us answer what we ourselves expect of Jesus. What does he *do* in our lives? The first way to answer these questions is to ask an additional one: "Where would the Expected One come from?" This is an important part of the historical puzzle, the chronological linkage between Old and New Testaments and the one that grants credibility to all that the prophets foresaw and all that we claim today.

In Old Testament times, the Israelites had a joint heir in Abraham, to whom God promised as many descendents as stars in the heavens (see Genesis 15). From Abraham's grandson Jacob, the lineage spread to the twelve tribes of Israel, each named for one of Jacob's sons. When this one large nation of Israel entered Canaan, they divided the land according to these twelve tribes. In time, the tribes consolidated politically into the northern kingdom of Israel and the southern kingdom of Judah, with Jerusalem as its capital. Yet all this while, the tribes were firm in their individual identities. A person would identify himself as from the tribe of Gad, or Reuben, even though he was an Israelite.

The pattern was the same as with modern genealogies, where branches of relatives are traced along the trunk of some long-deceased relative. The branches are all unified in the rootstock of that trunk. So, too, the Hebrew nation had a fierce loyalty to their tribe, but a common loyalty to their ancestors Abraham and Sarai. Especially during times of division and wars among tribes, certain prophets looked for someone who would restore the unity and enact the peace for the kingdom.

In their search for that special king, it is not surprising that Old Testament writers and prophets repeatedly refer to lineage. In fact, the first reference to a powerful ruler issuing from humankind itself to have dominion over evil is given by God himself. To the serpent in Eden, God ordains that the offspring of the woman "will strike your [Satan's] head" (Genesis 3:15), an act consummated by Jesus. Again, to Abraham God says that "and by your offspring shall all the nations of the earth gain blessing for themselves, because you have obeyed my voice" (Genesis 22:18). That sense of lineage appears from the beginning of God's Creation. It enforces the fact that God had a purpose, humanity thwarted it, but God will restore it.

Those facts are emphasized by Isaiah, the major prophet of the coming Messiah. Chapter 4 sets forth the development of the lineage to that time. Isaiah writes that "A shoot shall come out from the stump of Jesse, / and a branch shall grow out of his roots" (11:1). Essentially, he draws the family tree of the coming Redeemer, the one whom he called in chapter 9 both a "child" and "Mighty God." What will this Branch be like?

Isaiah lists some very specific traits. "The Spirit of the LORD shall rest on him," as Isaiah 11:2 tells us. That is, this Branch will not only arise out of Jesse, but he will also be specially anointed by the Spirit of God. Physically, this act occurred when John baptized Jesus and the voice from heaven announced: "You are my Son, the Beloved; with you I am well pleased" (Mark 1:11).

Among the further traits that Isaiah lists is "the Spirit of wisdom and understanding." *Wisdom* here is something far more than mere knowledge of facts. Knowledge can at times get in the way of wisdom and understanding. Wisdom sees behind things as they appear; it probes the deeper sources. But it also understands why things are the way they are. Those things of our lives that we don't understand, that just plain bewilder us, Jesus knows and understands.

Another trait that Isaiah gives to the Branch is "the Spirit of counsel and of power." Again, the words bear special significance for the anticipation of Jesus. In the Hebrew language, *counsel* suggests a kingly or royal administrative act. We still use the word with much that the same meaning today. But the word also suggests a deep and profound intimacy. We keep counsel with someone who knows us without any masks or secrets. The remarkable thing in Isaiah's prophecy is that Jesus knows us with rugged intimacy but also with the power to meet the needs of our intimacy.

The last part of Isaiah's vision of the Branch is that "the Spirit of knowledge and the fear of the Lord" will be with him. Again, I think that we can dismiss mere knowledge of facts as the quality suggested here, although surely Jesus—as God—had that, too. Jesus did not come into this world at Bethlehem and die on Golgotha to prove that 2 + 2 = 4. *Knowledge* as it is suggested here is the much more profound act of knowing the will of God. *Fear of the Lord,* on the other hand, is the way in which Jesus obeyed God's will.

Suddenly the genealogy seems important to me. Isaiah places Jesus as the most important Branch out of the "stump" of Jesse. But where does that leave us? Tomorrow we explore our place on the family tree.

Matthew 1:20–21

> "Joseph, son of David, do not be afraid to take Mary as your wife, for the child conceived in her is from the Holy Spirit. She will bear a son, and you are to name him Jesus, for he will save his people from their sins."

Prayer

Dear Lord, my true home, my true birthplace, is in you.
Thank you for your wisdom and understanding,
for your counsel and your power,
and for your knowledge and fear of God Almighty
—your Father and my God.
Teach me to love as you have loved,
to seek knowledge of your way,
to have the understanding of the Holy Spirit.
Bless me, I pray, with a Spirit
of wisdom and understanding,
of counsel and power,
of knowledge and the fear of the Lord.
Amen.

Third Saturday

THE BRANCH AND THE BANNER

How humble the term *The Branch* seems. How humble also the Branch of Jesus, born in some side-street stable of Bethlehem. Yet, like any branch, this one too can grow to a tremendous expanse, providing shady rest, protection, and quiet. That Branch born in Bethlehem grew, anointed by his Father with a Spirit of wisdom and understanding, of counsel and power, of knowledge and fear of the Lord.

Isaiah, however, continues the story of the Branch. This Branch grows new branches that will bring the same spirit across the face of the earth. In verse 10 of chapter 11, Isaiah proclaims: "In that day the Root of Jesse will stand as a banner for the peoples; the nations will rally to him, and his place of rest will be glorious" *(NIV)*. Several things important to us leap out of the verse.

First, Isaiah outlines the lineage. The root of Jesse is the human source for all these happenings. Jesse was the father of King David, the direct ancestor of Jesus. Matthew bases his entire gospel account on the authenticity of Jesus' lineage, except that he meticulously traces it all the way back to Abraham. Most important, however, Jesus himself claims that very lineage when he says in the Book of Revelation to John: "'It is I, Jesus, who sent my angel to you with this testimony for the churches. I am the root and the descendant of David, the bright morning star'" (22:16).

Isaiah emphasizes the "root of Jesse," but why does he refer to a "banner for the peoples" *(NIV)*? I think of the banners that hang in my church, this place where we are drawn together to worship. The banners direct our attention toward Christ whom we worship. He is the reason for our gathering. In this case, the banner is like the one mentioned in the Song of Songs. Here the beloved recalls how her lover has been with her, and in his presence she feels that "his banner over me is love" (2:4, *NIV*). In one sense, then, the banner suggests unity and love bestowed on us by our Lord. Through his infinite grace, Jesus "banners" us in love. On the sanctuary walls of our spiritual lives, he envelops us in banners that proclaim: "How very much I love you!"

The second, and more common, use of the banner in the Old Testament, however, is a signal of welcome. Such banners are familiar to us as well, staples of parades, festivals, grand openings, and the like.

Another verse from the Old Testament helps us make sense of this. When the Israelites entered the Desert of Sinai two years after leaving Egypt, God told Moses to undertake a census of the tribes. While in Egypt the tribes had been scattered by their masters. Now they needed a new structure as God's chosen people. Thus, Moses had the tribes spread out from the Tent of Meeting and gather according to tribes, "each man under his standard with the banner of his family" (Numbers 2:2, *NIV*). Thereby God imposed his order and identity upon the mass of people. As we draw together under the banner of Christ, we too are adopted from among the mass of humanity into the family of God. This is our joy and strength, and it echoes one more scene from ancient Israelite history.

When Moses defeated the enemy Amalekites, the first thing he did was build an altar of Thanksgiving. Exodus 17 reads: "Moses built an altar and called it, The LORD is my banner. He said, 'A hand upon the banner of the LORD! The LORD will have war with Amalek from generation to generation'" (v. 15). At the birth of Jesus the action is precisely reversed. Here the Lord reached down into humanity and set his banner of love over us.

Reach now, through time, to the very birth of Christ. Remember how those star-struck Magi saddled up their camels and rode toward Jerusalem? Or how those bedazzled shepherds ran their legs off to get to the stable? The Magi had the banner of a star leading them to Jesus. The shepherds had the banner of a choir of angels dancing on light. It was a gloryfest. Both appearances led the witnesses to the Banner of Christ. Largely ignored by the world at his birth, he is glorified by heavenly hosts and those who had their spiritual eyes wide open to the birth of Jesus.

When we think of Jesus as the Banner, we think first of a sign of protection and comfort over us. But especially during our advent, we look hard in a celebration of praise. The Magi set a straightforward course. The shepherds ran pell-mell to the stable. So too, we set our sights straight ahead to the joyful celebration of Jesus' birth.

Isaiah 62:10–11

Go through, go through the gates,
  prepare the way for the people;
build up, build up the highway,
  clear it of stones,
  lift up an ensign over the peoples.
The LORD has proclaimed
  to the end of the earth:
Say to daughter Zion,
  "See, your salvation comes;
his reward is with him,
  and his recompense before him."

Prayer

Thank you, Lord,
that your word is a lamp to my feet
and a light to my path.
In this life, my way
is often dimmed by detours
and confusion.
Answers seem as distant as stars.
Even then, especially then,
thank you that as I walk this path
your banner over me is love.
Amen.

Fourth Week in Advent

Fourth Sunday in Advent

LION OF JUDAH

The "Messiah" is still one of our most frequently used names for Jesus. Rightfully so, for we have seen that the name calls forth the expectations of one who delivers us. Moreover, that person (the Christ) will be anointed to his task of deliverance by none other than God himself. Then, finally, we witness the breathtaking miracle that the Messiah is in fact God himself.

No mere human being could enact the deliverance of all who turn to him. The means of that deliverance is prophesied already in Deuteronomy 21:23, where we read that "anyone hung on a tree is under God's curse." The Messiah endured God's curse so that we might escape it. Nor could any mere human being enact the resurrection for all who turn to him. Here the Messiah took back his crown of glory; he had done his work on earth and absolutely all that needed to be done. He ruptured not only the chains of sin but also the chains of time and mortality, opening the door for us on eternal life.

This is the Messiah King we celebrate at Advent. How do we begin to approach him? At the manger, surely, for that was the start of the miracle. But how do we measure the startling miracle that was his life, his death, and his resurrection? One way to grasp this is through the title "Lion of Judah."

The kingship of Jesus finds its roots in his nature as Creator. Jesus is fully man, but he is also fully God. As God is the Creator, so is Jesus. This important fact precedes all talk about his kingship. Scriptural passages may declare and describe Jesus' kingship, but their descriptions are based on Jesus' inherent nature. He is king before any man calls him king. His position depends neither on human recognition nor winning an election. His is an office anointed by God the Father from all eternity.

Matthew and Luke are careful in their gospels to trace Jesus' genealogy in the Davidic line in order to demonstrate his Messiahship. Yet, Jesus himself rejects this emphasis:

> *"How can the scribes say that the Messiah is the son of David? David himself, by the Holy Spirit, declared,*
> *'The Lord said to my Lord,*
> *"Sit at my right hand,*
> *until I put your enemies under your feet."'*
> *David himself calls him Lord; so how can he be his son?"*
>
> MARK 12:35–37

Jesus is not a lately ascended king. He is king—at once and forever.

To help us consider the unique qualities of Jesus' kingship, we might look at the Bible's curious and surprising association of the lion, the king of beasts, with the King of Man. In the Old Testament, this association is a frequent one.

The regality, nobility, and power of the lion are commonly noted facts in the Old Testament. God himself asks Job, "Can you hunt the prey for the lion, / or satisfy the appetite of the young lions?" (Job 38:39). Frequently, the lion is associated with a ruling authority, as in Proverbs 19:12, "A king's anger is like the growling of a lion."

Through the words of the prophet Jeremiah, God likens himself to the lion: "Like a lion coming up from the thickets of the Jordan" (Jeremiah 49:19) he will drive evildoers from the land. In Hosea, God compares himself to the lion—this time with reference to his rule over his chosen people: "For I will be like a lion to Ephraim, and like a young lion to the house of Judah" (Hosea 5:14). Hosea 11:10 repeats the theme:

They shall go after the LORD,
who roars like a lion;
when he roars,
his children shall come trembling.

The Old Testament image of the lion as the king of his people and the New Testament image of Jesus merge in Revelation 5:5, where Jesus is described specifically as "the Lion of the tribe of Judah, the Root of David." John has been weeping because not one of all the magnificent angelic creatures he has seen has the worth or inherent authority to open the Book of Life. The elder comforts him; there is One who has the necessary kingly authority, and it is Jesus.

The offspring of royal lineage, the root of David, and the King of all the redeemed merge in this one Jesus who alone is worthy to open the book of eternal life. The song of joy that bursts on John's ears is a ringing testimony: "To the one seated on the throne and to the Lamb / be blessing and honor and glory and might forever and ever!" (Revelation 5:13).

Hebrews 2:9

> [B]ut we do see Jesus, who for a little while was made lower than the angels, now crowned with glory and honor because of the suffering of death, so that by the grace of God he might taste death for everyone.

Prayer

With the angels and the redeemed of all the ages,
I proclaim glory and honor and power
to the King of Kings: Crown him Lord of all.
Lord, I don't know you
as the Lion of Judah,
but I do know you
as the king of all heaven and earth
and the one who rules my life.
I gladly give it to your keeping, Lord.
Amen.

Fourth Monday

MESSIAH: DESCENDANT OF DAVID

From the earliest pages of human history, God promised Jesus as the Redeemer. Throughout the Old Testament, people believed that the answer to God's promise would come through the political office of a Messiah. Although the exact term is used only twice in the entire Old Testament, this title of Jesus is rich in its implications to the Hebrew nation and dear in its fulfillment to the Christian church.

The title of Messiah is not part of the general fabric of our Christian life. The Hebrew word *Messiah* simply means "the anointed one." In the Gospels, the Hebrew word is given its Greek equivalent, *Christos,* or "Christ." Thus, every time we speak or think of Jesus as Christ we are, in effect, referring to Jesus as Messiah. It would be interesting to count the number of times the title of "Christ" is used in just one worship service. Each time, the word may as well be Messiah.

Those two times the title "Messiah" appears in the Old Testament occur in a vision of Daniel. Gabriel appears to Daniel while he is in deep prayer and says to him, "Daniel, I have now come out to give you wisdom and understanding. At the beginning of your supplications a word went out…consider the word and understand the vision" (9:22–23). Gabriel then goes on to interpret Daniel's vision. One part is explained as follows: "Know therefore and understand: from the time that the word went out to restore and rebuild Jerusalem until the time of an anointed prince..." (9:25). Then Gabriel gives numbers symbolic of the time between the restoration of Jerusalem (in the sixth century BC) and the advent of the Messiah. But, further, Gabriel, speaking from the mystery of God's knowledge, says that the "anointed one shall be cut off and shall have nothing" (9:26). With the benefit of hindsight, we understand this to be the crucifixion—the Messiah hung on a cross, cut off from everyone, even his heavenly Father.

These passages are fairly complicated Scripture. Most visions and prophecies are, and few scholars presume to understand them fully. What clearly emerges here, nonetheless, is the expectation of a Messiah who will, cruelly and mysteriously, be "cut off."

The messianic nature of Jesus, then, is a profound and living aspect of the Christ we worship. As Jesus was, so he is, and so he continues to be in the future. To discover this, we explore further the roots of the title "Messiah," or Christ.

From the earliest passages of the Old Testament to the last, the idea of a Messiah is expressed. In its early stages, the concept is largely that of a deliverer with a prophetic role—one who would clearly and truthfully relate God's will. With the establishment of the kings over Israel, however, the title assumes a distinctly royal, authoritative bearing associated with the lineage of David. Gabriel's revelation also takes place in this context.

A subtle historical point appears here. Recall that the people of Israel demanded a king to rule over them. They wanted to be "like other nations" (1 Samuel 8:5). When Samuel intercedes with God, the Lord makes it clear that "they have not rejected you, but they have rejected me from being king over them" (1 Samuel 8:7). This is a key point: Saul, the king approved by the people, represents the people's rejection of God as their present king. God gave them what they wanted. Saul was outstanding, tall, handsome—a king who met the people's criteria. But the Messiah will be God's choice, and then once again God will rule his people.

Why did God select the lineage of David for the future Messiah? Because David, unlike Saul, was God's choice of a replacement. Jesse, David's father, did not even think it worthwhile to call David in from the fields to meet Samuel. This young shepherd couldn't be king! Yet, this was God's choice—the humble shepherd. God will work through whomever he will.

As merely a human king, David's reign is wracked by sin and sorrow. Still, as God's anointed, King David exemplified many traits that would also mark the Messiah to come.

First, David showed great mercy, not only on the poor and oppressed, but even on his enemies. Several times the life of Saul lay in David's hand, and he refused to squeeze it out.

Second, David was a worshipful king who sought, through his own human frailty, to honor the God who chose him. The Psalms in particular bear eloquent witness to David's respect and love for God.

Third, David sought justice in his kingdom. Although his sinful, human nature led him to commit unjust acts, David was keenly aware of the times he violated God's standards, and he labored to rule as a fair king.

In these ways—mercy, worship, and justice—David suggests, but only suggests, the nature of the Messiah who was to come and rule as king.

1 John 3:23

> And this is his commandment, that we should believe in the name of his Son Jesus Christ and love one another, just as he has commanded us.

Prayer

In this Advent season, Lord,
prevent me from bowing the knee
to the malls and gifts and glitter.
Like David, I pray that
"You will create in me a clean heart,"
so that when I bow before the altar,
I may be blessed by my Messiah,
my Redeemer, Deliverer, Lord, and King.
Amen.

Fourth Tuesday

THE WOUNDED KING

There is a passage in Isaiah that...well, just bothers me enormously. It is couched right in the middle of a description of the work of the Messiah, then it falls like a thud. Everything sounds offkey.

Perhaps you have been at a party where something occurs that throws everything out of step. The smile becomes a struggle. People start looking for coats. Everyone is deeply uncomfortable.

The passage—a brief line, really, only six words long—creeps out of Isaiah 53:5: "By his wounds we are healed" *(NIV).*

I, probably like many others, read over the line quickly, perhaps enjoying its place in the poetry of the chapter. But then it seems to snag you, like the briars of a rose. It holds you fast—Do you see what I'm saying here?

"By his wounds we are healed."

The words bother me because I just can't seem to grasp the full meaning.

Please join me while I try to think this through, while I try to fit this huge mystery, this miracle, into the small confines of my life.

First, I must acknowledge that everything—*everything*—we explore about Advent is something we are also exploring about Jesus' death on Golgotha. Jesus did not enter this world as an infant merely to pull some miraculous tricks as a man. Nor did he go to the cross just to have his life snuffed out. Please. Jesus entered this world *because of* the cross. His destination was the very reason for his coming.

This in itself is miracle enough. But how about our healing and the wounds by which we are healed?

I want to be very careful how I say this. There must be no misunderstanding. *"By his wounds"*—who laid those bruises on our King, the Messiah? Well, we might say that the Roman soldiers did. After all, it's right there in the gospel account. But that is not quite accurate. Those Roman soldiers were the agents of our sins inflicted on the Messiah. If God has our names engraved in the palm of his hand (see Isaiah 49:16), then just as surely our hands were on the whips that wounded our king. This was Jesus' divine appointment, set from all eternity, set in motion in a manger in Bethlehem.

This I know to be true; yet, it still does not seem to fully unwrap the mystery of those words, *"By his wounds we are healed."* Yes, the spiritual healing of our sin-sick souls occurred right there—through the suffering of our King. But there is more to the story of the bruises.

Few of us escape those moments when suffering thuds into our lives like an unruly guest. Suddenly the guest runs roughshod over our lives and the guests, our comforters, scramble toward the exits.

Those wounds land not on our backs but on our hearts. The world no longer makes sense. Nothing does. Perhaps even our relationship with Jesus no longer makes sense. We mouth the universal plea through dry lips: How could this happen to me? And why?

Here is the miracle of the manger. We can lay those very personal wounds also upon our King. *By his wounds, we are healed.* Notice that that verb is in the present tense. It isn't only something that occurred on a mount called Golgotha when the wounded King healed us, once and for all, of our sin. Rather, this soul-healing is an ongoing action. Jesus was emphatic when he said to his disciples, and to us: "Peace I leave with you; my peace I give to you. I do not give to you as the world gives. Do not let your hearts be troubled, and do not let them be afraid" (John 14:27).

In his peace, we can take those inner wounds, *our* heart wounds, and give them to Jesus. The outstretched arms of the infant in Bethlehem grew to be the outstretched arms of our Savior on the cross.

John 15:18–19

"If the world hates you, be aware that it hated me before it hated you. If you belonged to the world, the world would love you as its own. Because you do not belong to the world, but I have chosen you out of the world."

Prayer

Thank you, Holy Savior,
Jesus, my Wounded King.
You came into this world
as a helpless infant;
you died helpless on the cross.
And why, dear Lord?
Here is the mystery—
the majesty of divine love
that took my sins upon you,
and placed your Spirit within me;
the mercy of your eternal love
which heals all my wounds.
Amen.

Fourth Wednesday

DRAWING NEAR: THE QUIET CENTER

Be still, and know that I am God!

These words from Psalm 46:10 challenge us to the very center of our being. The words are a command: *You be still.* They come with a promise: *and know that I am God.* The two—being still and knowing God—work together.

How do we get down to that center core of our lives? Then to be quiet there?

As one means, many Christians are turning to the very old practice of labyrinth prayer. The labyrinth is not to be mistaken with a maze, a source of disconcerting confusion. Some of these are cut into cornfields when the corn towers high and you seem always to run into dead ends. It may be a fun adventure, but it is also bewildering, even a bit frightening.

The prayer labyrinth is different, and much treasured in Christian tradition. Several cathedrals built in Europe during the Middle Ages had a labyrinth built into the pattern of the floor. One such was the famous cathedral at Chartres, France.

How does the labyrinth prayer work? It is a thoughtful walk, but a walk inward to thoughts of God. The labyrinth is no more than a path of concentric circles leading to a quiet center for prayerful meditation. The labyrinth may appear in a church building or outside in a grassy space, often bordered by flowers and shrubs. There is nothing "magical" about the design or place. The labyrinth prayer is simply a physical means—like a retreat or secluded meditation—to a spiritual end: communion with the Lord who reigns over time and place.

The idea of the labyrinth as a physical means is that as we walk inward we leave behind the cares of this world that tug and twist at us. We arrive at a quiet center where we can be still and know that our Savior is Lord. After the refreshing time with God, we walk out, as we always must, to the world in which God has placed us.

How, then, does the labyrinth prayer relate to Advent? This we know: God has come to the very center of our lives. Jesus was born so that when we are still, we can know that he is Lord. Jesus has already drawn close to us, and now he waits for us to draw close to him. That is the great, good news—the gospel—that Advent echoes across the rooftops.

As we move inward on that path to the quiet center, we divest ourselves of the ordinary. We set aside on the path our many separate roles in this world and appear before Jesus "just as I am." That is, after all, just how he loves you, not because you are a pediatrician, an accountant, or a wife or a husband. Leave behind your anger, your fear, even your sense that you are not appreciated by others. Jesus appreciates you so much that he left the splendor of heaven for you.

At the center we take a great risk. We let ourselves be known to Jesus. We give ourselves over to him, completely emptying our drives and desires, our pleasure and pain, our ambition and failure, so that his presence may fill those spaces. We also listen. We wait. We give Jesus the opportunity to speak. His voice may come quickly and clearly. It may not be fully comprehended until much later. But be still. Listen.

God has called us to be in the world, so we do have to leave again. We walk the same path, smell the same flowers, see the same shrubs. We are leaving now. We think of what God would have us take back into the world. But then we know. It is the gift given to us again at Advent—the joy of our Savior's birth.

The labyrinth prayer does not have to take place in some physical place at all. Indeed, it is a path we take when we are still. We look inward, separating ourselves for a time from the world's hold on us. Being still, we make the space and time to know that Jesus is Lord.

2 Peter 3:18

But grow in the grace and knowledge of our Lord and Savior Jesus Christ. To him be the glory both now and to the day of eternity. Amen.

Prayer

Dear Lord, Prince of Peace,
may the quiet assurance of your presence
come upon me now.
Each day, I pray, may I walk a path
where you are at the center.
I know that when I leave
I never leave alone.
As you spoke to your disciples
so you speak to me:
"Remember, I am with you always,
to the end of the age" (Matthew 28:20).
Amen.

Fourth Thursday

DRAWING NEAR: HEROIC FAITH

My children grew up in the age of the superhero action figures—The Incredible Hulk, Superman, "Spidey," and the like. Then *Star Wars* came along and suddenly weirdly shaped creatures packed every nook and cranny of the toy boxes. Occasionally, my two grandsons still pull some out of the toy closet today.

All of these heroes, as I remember it, had "special" powers to combat injustice. That is why they were called *super*heroes. We humans are all too human. Our powers are not very powerful. I think that is why one special person from the Bible has always inspired me as a hero of faith.

She was an unassuming young woman; an orphan, in fact, being raised by her cousin.

She didn't seem to think too highly of herself, even though Hebrew tradition tells us that she was one of the three most beautiful women that ever lived—right there with Eve (who was formed by God's fingertips), and Bathsheba (who was so beautiful she turned King David's head into a loop). That's what tradition tells us.

We know her only as a young woman named Hadassah (meaning "myrtle"), living around the time of 480 BC. Her Gentile or Persian name, since she and her cousin were living in exile in Persia, was Esther (meaning "star"). There seemed to be nothing at all unusual with our young Jewish girl Esther—then her world turned upside down.

In brief, King Xerxes held a drunken banquet for his noblemen. His queen, Vashti, held a similar banquet for the leading ladies. Near the end of the feasting, Xerxes called for Vashti to come and parade her beauty for his drunken nobles. She refused, an unbelievable affront to the divine authority of the king. With the encouragement of his closest advisors, Xerxes deposed her.

As happens in these matters, Xerxes yearned for a new queen. He decided that a national beauty pageant would be just the thing, so he called all the beautiful young women of the kingdom to undergo a yearlong preparation in beauty school and then parade before Xerxes. Esther, we might say in today's language, scored perfect 10s before the king and his advisors. A new queen was found.

At that very time, one of the king's advisors, a weasel named Haman, undertook his personal ambition to rid the kingdom of Jews—and to keep their wealth, of course. There was one unexpected snag in his plan, however. That was Esther, for she was a Jew.

When Mordecai informed Esther of the plot, she had a choice to make. She alone could intercede with the king. No other Jew was close enough; no one else could possibly access the king's attention. But the king had not seen her for over a month. Maybe he no longer wanted to see her. Moreover, if someone appeared in the throne room and the king was not in the mood to see that person, he would not hold out the golden scepter of welcome. That person was immediately taken to execution. Not surprisingly, Esther did not rush headlong to the king to plead her case. This was a fearful situation. Instead, she asked Mordecai and all the Jews to pray and fast with her for three days.

Do you remember those immortal words of Mordecai, urging her on? He said:

> *"For if you keep silence at such a time as this, relief and deliverance will rise for the Jews from another quarter, but you and your father's family will perish. Who knows? Perhaps you have come to royal dignity for just such a time as this."*
>
> ESTHER 4:14

Esther, we must understand, was not the only person to be challenged in such a way.

At a stony, threatening time in history, Jesus came to just such a time as this. His coming wasn't just once and for all at Bethlehem, it was for all history and forever. Just as Esther's decision changed the course of history for the Jews, Jesus' decision to be born in human flesh changed the course of all history for all humanity forever.

But why, exactly, do I call Esther one of the great heroes of faith? And what exactly is a hero of faith? Are you one?

We'll explore that further in tomorrow's meditation.

Isaiah 53:2–3

> [H]e had no form or majesty that we should look at him,
> nothing in his appearance that we should desire him.
> He was despised and rejected by others;
> a man of suffering and acquainted with infirmity;
> and as one from whom others hide their faces
> he was despised, and we held him of no account.

Prayer

I confess, Lord, that I am afraid
of a great many things.
I am no hero; that I know.
It seems sometimes that I have
no spiritual legs to stand on.
My confession is that I am not worthy,
you know this, Lord.
Yet you love me, Lord.
I know your word is forever true.
Please forgive me,
scrape out those sins I cling to
in my most secret heart,
and anoint me with the healing oil
of your boundless grace.
Amen.

Fourth Friday

DRAWING NEAR: STANDING FIRM IN FAITH

We know the rest of Esther's heroic story. She did make her lonely journey, all alone to the throne room. She stood in the gap for all her people when, as Xerxes reached out his golden scepter, she made her request before him.

We know that evil was thwarted, that Haman himself was hanged on the seventy-five-foot gallows he had erected to hang Mordecai and other Jews. We know that the Jews were given special rights in the kingdom to celebrate their own religious festivals. Among these was the newly instituted feast of Purim, a time of unparalleled rejoicing.

At such a time as this, Esther stood firm.

The parallels should be obvious. Jesus came into this world and made his lonely journey, all alone, to the cross. Even God, his father, seemed to have abandoned him: "My God, my God, why have you forsaken me?" (Matthew 27:46). Only the Son of God could stand in the gap, crush evil itself, and give deliverance to his people. And because Jesus did this, we have the blessed expectation of the joyful wedding feast in heaven.

But a hero of faith? Is that only for Esther and Jesus? Does the title apply only to those giants of faith in the Bible—Abraham, David, Paul, John?

What are some of the characteristics of a hero of faith? I think I could build a list from here to Australia, simply because I fall short of so many of the qualities. but I'll just give four.

First, the hero of faith has complete confidence. Especially in eternal matters, for these come from God. For example, Jesus said, "I am the resurrection and the life. Those who believe in me, even though they die, will live, and everyone who lives and believes in me will never die" (John 11:25–26). I don't know this rationally, since it lies beyond my experiences. But I do have complete confidence that so it shall be, because Jesus said so.

Second, why does the hero of faith have such confidence? Because its source is in God. Because God said it, I will believe it. His word is eternal, certain, and unchanging. King Solomon put it like this:

> *Trust in the LORD with all your heart,*
> *and do not rely on your own insight.*
> *In all your ways acknowledge him,*
> *and he will make straight your paths.*
>
> *PROVERBS 3:5–6*

The hero of faith has confidence, and the source of that confidence is trust in God.

The third quality of the hero of faith is being called to action. We remember Mordecai's words to Esther: "at such a time as this." Now is the time for action. The hero of faith never disappears into the woodwork. The hero has a task much like Esther's—to redeem the world, to work to save God's people…"at such a time as this."

Finally, the hero of faith is not conformed to this world. Yes, Jesus died for this world. Yes, we are called to redeem the world, even courageously and sacrificially. But the world is not our home. We have another destination. We are traveling to the Promised Land. In his letter to the Colossians, Paul writes, "See to it that no one takes you captive through philosophy and empty deceit, according to human tradition, according to the elemental spirits of the universe, and not according to Christ" (2:8). Instead, Paul tells us in 2 Corinthians 10:5 that we "we take every thought captive to obey Christ."

But, we ask again, is this heroic faith reserved only for the likes of Esther, David, Jesus, and Paul? Here is the amazing thing. When we confess Jesus, this newborn king, as Lord of our lives, *we* are heroes of faith. We have testified to our complete confidence in him; we trust God's word that he is the Son of God born in a manger. We have acted on our trust by acknowledging him Lord of our lives. We are converted, turned from this world to the City of God.

Our final challenge on this Advent journey of drawing closer to Jesus is to understand ourselves as sons and daughters of the king. A final look at Esther's heroic faith tomorrow helps us make that step.

Hebrews 11:1

> Now faith is the assurance of things hoped for, the conviction of things not seen.

Prayer

Dear Lord, there will be a time
when my faith will be sight.
Jesus my Savior will descend
with the trumpet call
as the clouds roll back
on his shining glory,
and I'll bend the knee
and say, I have seen Jesus!
Amen.

Fourth Saturday

DRAWING NEAR: COMMON HEROES

There is little question about Esther's heroic faith.

When everything stood against her, she stood firm.

When the threat of unexpected action warranted death, she acted.

When her greatest enemy, Haman, posed a threat of danger to all her people, she destroyed his evil.

When the truth had to be told, even against all good reason, she spoke the truth.

There are times when the truth is not reasonable. At times, truth can stand against all the "reasonable" claims and standards of this world. A queen does not approach the throne of the fearsome Xerxes.

Where do we take our stand, how do we act, when do we denounce evil, how do we speak the truth? We have another model for our faith life. Esther was born into humble circumstances, to a Jewish people held in captivity. Jesus was born in lowly conditions, to a humble artisan and a young maiden. Jesus too was born to a people held in captivity—the bondage of sin. As Esther stood for her people at her place and time, Jesus stood for all people, at all places, and for all time.

Esther stood firm against the threat to her people. Jesus stood firm in his task. While Esther faced the threat of death, Jesus knew that his death was the sole purpose for his life. Esther spoke the truth when the truth counted most. Lives depended on her. Jesus is the truth, the way, the life (see John 14:6). Haman threatened everything Esther believed in, and by the risk of her action she destroyed him. Satan shadows this world seeking those whom he may devour (see 1 Peter 5:8), including the Prince of Peace. By his action, Jesus crushed the serpent's power.

But you and I—are we heroes? I'm not. Sometimes I seem to bumble along through this world, falling down, scraping my knees. Sometimes they are too bruised to kneel in prayer.

Remember that Esther and Jesus came from the most humble of earthly beginnings. Remember that David was a shepherd boy, that Moses stuttered so badly he had to have Aaron speak for him, that Peter once denied his Lord, that Paul was once Saul.

Consider an analogy. In the tradition of fairy tales several traits are common. In fact, they define the genre. For example, among these traits is the fact that the lead characters are perfectly ordinary, often children. Furthermore, they are called to do tasks they never thought imaginable. They travel on a quest to find a precious object or person. Most often the trials on the quest come with great danger. The characters often wonder why they ever started on this quest. But as they forge onward, they discover "helpers" who assist them in overcoming the threat. Having overcome, the characters—and this is a necessity—live happily ever after.

Perhaps it was the nature of these traits that led the Christian author J. R .R. Tolkien—writer of *The Lord of the Rings*—to declare that the Bible is the world's greatest fairy story. I imagine this claim met with some outrage. But for Tolkien, as for his friend C. S. Lewis, all fairy stories point to the truth, and the Bible is the truth itself (see the Tolkien essay "On Faerie Stories"). You see, it is our story, and the greatest story ever told.

We are the common characters who undertake the quest to Bethlehem this Advent. We don't come with any special powers of our own, and surely nothing that merits our coming. But we do journey with the divine help of the Holy Spirit, whose Bright Morning Star constantly illuminates our way. Surely we may find dangers along the way, even the threat of detours that can lead us astray. But at the end of the journey, on Christmas morning, we find the most precious object and person imaginable. Our Savior, Jesus, is born to us this day. And that it the happiest ending that we can ever dream of.

Luke 2:13–14

> And suddenly there was with the angel a multitude of the heavenly host, praising God and saying,
> “Glory to God in the highest heaven,
> and on earth peace among those whom he favors!”

Prayer

Jesus, thank you for the dawning of joy
that came with the birth
of the one true Light,
the Light of the World,
that appeared in Bethlehem
that terrific morning.
Glory shone all around.
Jesus, that is my destination
again this Advent.
Lead me by your Holy Spirit,
protect me by your power,
so that I might arrive safely
into your perfect, and everlasting, peace.
Amen.

Christmas

Christmas

AT THE QUIET CENTER

And now our expectations are at the full. Our Advent journey nears completion. It may be today. It may be tomorrow, depending on the yearly calendar.

Except that now, for the first time, we call it by another name—Christmas. The name comes from two Old English words: *Christes* and *mæsse,* the feast or festival for Christ. Indeed, it is time for celebration. The Messiah has come. Joy to the world! What a wondrous story of love.

If we turn our eyes on the world, it may indeed seem like a hopeless place—a tiny dot in the cosmos where little lives flicker briefly against the darkness.

For the past decade, my wife has delivered meals to shut-ins through an organization called "God's Kitchen." When she picks up meals in the morning, it is customary to have the lost and homeless propped against the building as they wait for something to eat. They seem to have lost all hope of restoration.

We look at the world around us, where wars and rumors of wars rage. We can put a finger nearly anywhere on the map and find conflict there. All hope for peace seems lost.

And sometimes we look deep within ourselves, and find our own hopes and dreams in shattered ruins—like pieces of burned glass that can never be fused together. We battle illness, tragedy, sometimes just plain despair. Past the gray walls, we try to glimpse hope.

Be still and know: your hope has come.

Think back to God's first Christmas announcement in Genesis 3:15. How the ancient people must have looked forward to Jesus' coming. The problem is they already had defined to the Giver the gift they wanted; their Messiah conformed to their shopping list. When the real Messiah appeared, they didn't even recognize him.

Their blindness was not for a lack of adequate signs. Over and over, God sent signs and wonders directing people to the One who was to come. The voices of the prophets rose in chorus. Isaiah cried out, "Listen, you that are deaf; / and you that are blind, look up and see!" (42:18). The signs were all about. The prophecies abundantly pointed to a coming Savior.

In our time, we too run the risk of having a world run wild with commercialized havoc drowning out the quiet space that permits Jesus a door to our hearts. For just a few moments at least, we need to whisper "Be still my soul."

Indeed, the journey through Advent sometimes reminds me of the ways we can take a vacation trip. Sometimes we need a vacation afterward just to recover from the trip. Sometimes we want to drive toward Christmas with the cruise control set at five miles per hour over the speed limit, stopping once every three hours for a quick break. Slow down. Let the quiet and the celebration of Christmas come to you.

I am thinking in particular of the way we go to the cabin we rent in the western mountains of North Carolina, right by the Cherokee Reservation. It is just outside Maggie Valley to be precise, but precious few people have ever heard of that little town tucked among the hills. I remember the first time we went to "our" cabin.

The best way to cross over into North Carolina from Tennessee is by side roads. The blatting tires of semis on Interstate 40 from Knoxville to Asheville drown out that feeling of going inward to the living heart of the mountains. One needs the curves and valleys, the strong heights that come as they may, to get there.

Many years earlier my wife and I were on our honeymoon, winding our way over these same roads. We were following Civil War battlefields across southern Tennessee and into North Carolina then. Today my son and his friend are in the back of the van studying the latest prices of basketball cards in their new *Beckett,* my daughter and her husband are following in their car, and our passage is more civil and less warlike. We come seeking peace with ourselves and the land.

Still, we take the side roads, south of I-40 on U.S. Route 321, then across the gap into Maggie Valley. Maggie Valley is the sweet sister of Gatlinburg, Tennessee. In Gatlinburg, elbows knock you at every turn, country and western music blares from loudspeakers on the main street, and smog lies as thick as a merchant's wallet. In Maggie Valley, you have room to breathe, people take their sweet time to talk, life slows down. The only other couple in the ice cream shop in the main square on this day appears to be newlyweds. She leans toward him and says softly, "I love you, Chuckie-Poo." He grins. "I love you too, Maggie-Pie."

Our cabin is still further into the mountains. The road switchbacks are like coiled rope. The last half-mile uphill is a crawl in low gear. Before we unpack, though, we sit for a while on the porch swing and chairs. Plenty of time to unpack.

Clouds drape the face of the mountain across from us. "Look," I say, "the clouds here fall up." Yes, they do. For rain has started in the valley now and long strings of confetti clouds are tugged upward by God's hand.

But on this day I don't look too long at the clouds dancing in thermal drafts, nor at the opposing mountains. Only on sunny days does one's vision stretch outward. On gray days, and now with the rain brushing softly on leaves around the cabin, and then with duller plopping sounds on the roof, one looks in close. Instead of the trees stacked vertically in the distance, one notices the tangle of yellow flowers around those stones over there. Standing amid a bunch of wild raspberry, the flowers have pale, five-petalled clusters with a puff of stamen like the gold in heirloom brooches. And now, low to the ground as if they are too shy for their taller cousins, a tiny flower with cupped petals the color of periwinkle sky. I go to my knees to see it, my clothes wet against the moss.

Right across the path an infinite variety of green leaves of hickory and sassafras and other trees that I can't name hang heavy with the rain, but I don't look that far. Not now.

It is a day for looking close. And close to my heart.

Sometimes this looking inward can bear the pain of a twist drill curving inward, peeling away the husks that can wrap a heart. But today it is an act of discovering a sweetness too long lost under those husks. Like driving from Gatlinburg to Maggie Valley.

This is the sweetness that slowing down brings.

As you and I stand on the threshold of Christmas, it is a time for renewing our vows, for remembering festival and joy. But it is also a time for remembering our deliverance. Stand there, let the quiet of the Messiah's love fall on you like a soft summer rain. Listen to his whisper to you, his bride or groom: "I love you. I will never leave you nor forsake you." That's his vow to us at Christmas.

John 15:11

> "I have said these things to you so that my joy may be in you, and that your joy may be complete."

Prayer

> I wait quietly now, Lord.
> Right in the middle
> of festival, let me hear
> your voice saying that
> your joy, in me,
> is complete.
> Thank you for that joy that never ends,
> and that no darkness can ever touch.
> *Amen.*